♪

# *Do You Hear What I Hear?*

♫

The Life and Teaching Career of
Marge Rivingston

Order this book online at www.trafford.com/07-0424
or email orders@trafford.com

Most Trafford titles are also available at major online book retailers.

Cover Design/Artwork by Dick Brevoort

Note for Librarians: A cataloguing record for this book is available from Library
and Archives Canada at www.collectionscanada.ca/amicus/index-e.html

Printed in Victoria, BC, Canada.

ISBN: 978-1-4251-2020-7

*We at Trafford believe that it is the responsibility of us all, as both individuals
and corporations, to make choices that are environmentally and socially sound.
You, in turn, are supporting this responsible conduct each time you purchase a
Trafford book, or make use of our publishing services. To find out how you are
helping, please visit www.trafford.com/responsiblepublishing.html*

*Our mission is to efficiently provide the world's finest, most comprehensive
book publishing service, enabling every author to experience success.
To find out how to publish your book, your way, and have it available
worldwide, visit us online at www.trafford.com/10510*

 www.trafford.com

**North America & international**
toll-free: 1 888 232 4444 (USA & Canada)
phone: 250 383 6864 ♦ fax: 250 383 6804 ♦ email: info@trafford.com

**The United Kingdom & Europe**
phone: +44 (0)1865 487 395 ♦ local rate: 0845 230 9601
facsimile: +44 (0)1865 481 507 ♦ email: info.uk@trafford.com

10  9  8  7  6  5  4

# Foreword

*The study of music is vast. Singing, while only
a small part of the musical spectrum, is peculiar
in that the voice you are born with determines
your sound, and you can't send it back if you
don't like its tone. You can, however, improve
it past all recognition, and past what you yourself
thought possible, and that is Marge Rivingston's gift.*

*Marge has taught singing for nearly forty years, and
she knows her stuff. Her method is clear, easy to
understand and reproduce, and she gets results. She
draws on both the oldest and the latest in thought
about vocal production, and somehow manages to be
encouraging and upbeat even on a singer's darkest,
most panic-stricken days.*

*Marge has trained some of the most beautiful voices of
my generation. I had such a great time with her, and I
am delighted that this book is now available to others
who are looking for guidance.*

Bette Midler

# Prologue

As I have thought about how to begin this book of my life in and around the theater, it occurred to me that it is still a large mystery how it all transpired. The beginning is the obvious place to start, so together we will take this journey that covers my life from birth to age seventy plus.

It is an overview of the wonderful times and experiences that I have been lucky enough to have over this life span. I continue to have wonderful experiences but on a less consistent basis, and that is certainly appropriate for my life now. There are always new and wonderful things to learn. (One of them is the ability to operate this computer. Who would have thought thirty or forty years ago that this technology was a possibility?)

So, come along with me on this journey, and picture in your mind the stages and the props that I used to create these memories.

The book contains four parts:
- My autobiography
- A narrative of lessons in singing
- Appendix of vocal exercises
- The enclosed CD

# Acknowledgements

**Tony Schillaci** for the title of this book.

**Kathryn Lowe** for her copyediting and for creating form out of what I had written.

**Kathryn Marie Bild** for proofing, refining and defining.

**Kimberly Mendiola** for pictures and layout and total support.

**Taylor Barton** for proofing and sharing her knowledge of how to make the CD work.

**Deborah Johnson** for suggestions in the exercise section and being the one to let me hear them with her voice.

**Dick Brevoort** for his fabulous illustrations for the cover.

**My students** for their support during this whole long process.

Gratitude to **Bette Midler** for the foreword and permission to use her name on the cover.

**Karla De Vito** for the initial idea of getting my work out there.

All those who contributed glowing quotes of their work with me.

**Personal friends** who have supported this idea and lived with it for years.

**Bill Schneider** for all his expertise in producing the CD.

**Allison Moffett** for mastering the CD.

**Laurel Masse** for the female vocals and **Bruce Eckstut** for the male vocals.

**Bill Goltman** for his computer skills in making sure I didn't lose vital statistics.

**Dr. Daniel Truong** for keeping my voice workable for teaching and sharing with others.

**Nancy Rayl** for her expert help and advice in editing this book.

Some good laughter along the way, mainly me wondering why I ever thought I could write a book. So credit to me too.

This book could not have happened without all of them.

# List of Students I Have Been Privileged to Teach

Kaye Ballard
Jim Belushi
Robby Benson
Barry Bostwick
Kate Burton
Kate Capshaw
Dixie Carter
Rosanne Cash
Shaun Cassidy
Patrick Cassidy
David Cassidy
Tim Curry
Rodney Crowell
Robert De Niro
Karla De Vito
Julia Louis Dreyfus
Faye Dunaway
Christine Ebersole
Carrie Fisher
Lesley Gore
Ellen Greene
Andy Gibb
Harry Groener
Mary Gross
Mark Hamill
Corky Hale
Emmylou Harris
George Irving

Bill Irwin
Glynis Johns
Madeline Kahn
Lila Kedrova
Kevin Kline
Ron Liebman
Natasha Makarova
Maureen McGovern
Bette Midler
Larry Moss
Peter Noone
Phyllis Newman
Sarah Jessica Parker
Estelle Parsons
Jane Powell
Anthony Quinn
Peter Riegert
Linda Ronstadt
Annie Ross
Elizabeth Shue
Rex Smith
Meryl Streep
James Taylor
Treat Williams
Paxton Whitehead
Michael York
Stephanie Zimbalist
And many more

Maureen McGovern, Singer with the Stradivarius Voice! (2/2/07)

*They say "when the student is ready, the teacher will appear." Well, Marge Rivingston came into my life in 1981 as a part of my Broadway "Pirates of Penzance" contract. At the time, I was a 30-year-old self-taught pop singer who thought, "I've taught myself to sing, thank-you-very-much. I don't want to end up sounding like one of those opera divas with a mile-wide vibrato reminiscent of the ghost of Bert Lahr!" Boy, was I mistaken!*

*For the past 26 years, Marge has been my singing coach. She has helped me to expand my vocal range and to develop greater breath control and vocal stamina. With a laser beam precision, she instantly zeros in on a problem and fixes it. She is a great teacher and a great friend. She always shows the way.*

David Friedman, Conductor & Songwriter Extraordinaire! (1/28/07)

*Marge Rivingston was my first and most important mentor in the art of teaching singing. Not only does she teach solid technique, but she has a marvelous way of guiding her students through the emotional and technical pitfalls of building a voice and building a career. There is no better asset and support system than having Marge by your side as you navigate the waters of show business.*

Christine Ebersole, Star and Tony Winner of Broadway Musicals  (2/2/07)

*My vocal technique was a mess until I met up with Marge Rivingston and her magical musical powers. Through studying with her, she taught me the skills and technique to integrate my 3½-octave range. When anyone asks me how I learned to sing like that, I say, "It is God & Marge Rivingston."*

Dixie Carter (2/5/07)

*Marge has had a wonderful career as a singer and singing teacher. She gives her students her technical expertise, her musical and artistic insights, and her heart as well.*

Robby Benson & Karla De Vito (2/20/07)

*If it hadn't been for the experience of Marge Rivingston, I never would have been able to sing the part of Frederic in the "Pirates of Penzance" on Broadway.*

*I am a natural baritone, and singing a tenor role 8 times a week seemed impossible. Marge Rivingston took my battered voice and 'magically' turned an insecure actor/once-singer into someone who could actually sing and move the show forward and concentrate on my comic timing rather than the "B" flats. I can't speak for others although I know this to be true: she is the best at what she does; she is a vocal miracle-worker. I will always be indebted to Ms. Rivingston because she also gave me the voice to propose to my Mabel, Karla De Vito, another student of hers (who is the real deal), and this Frederic and Karla's Mabel have been happily married now for 25 years. I believe Ms. Rivingston's magic had something to do with that bliss as well.*

~~~~~~~~~~

Estelle Parsons (3/1/07)

*Studying with Marge Rivingston was a joy and a delight. Her vast musical knowledge, warmth and positive feedback make a lesson a great adventure.*

~~~~~~~~~~

Rosanne Cash (3/12/07)

*Marge Rivingston introduced me to my own voice. I didn't have a clue who I was as a singer, or how to get better, until I started working with Marge in the early 1980's. She has had a profound and lasting impact on me. I owe her a great debt.*

~~~~~~~~~~

Treat Williams (4/8/07)

*I remember my trips to West End Avenue to see Marge Rivingston with great fondness. Her guidance and coaching were invaluable to me when I did Pirates of Penzance and I will always be grateful for her help.*

~~~~~~~~~~

George Cole (London) (5/18/07)

*I didn't believe I could sing until Marge Rivingston finished with me in "Pirates."*

*Marge, I don't know whether you were with us on the first day we moved into the theatre with the orchestra. An example of my musical innocence. I was called for two o'clock. I went down to the stage: here is the conversation with Bill Elliott, the Conductor.*

Bill: Hi, George.
Me:  Hallo, Bill.

Bill: Right after four, George.
Me:  (Exiting)

Bill: Where are you going?
Me:  To get a cup of tea. You said "After four."

Bill: No, George, after a *count* of four. OK?
Me:  Ah.

Bill: Right – two-three-four.
Me:  Hang on, Bill. What happened to one?

(George was assigned to me to teach him how to sing the part of the Major General.)

# ♪ Chapter One ♫

## Early Life and Education

*"A work of art is a corner of creation
seen through a temperament"*
*~Emile Zola*

♪

*Little Marge*

A t a little after midnight on December 4, 1927, I was born in Santa Ana, California. It was a night when the Santa Ana winds were blowing mightily, and according to my mother, I entered this world yelling my head off. My observation after seventy years is that I never have stopped howling. What we can attribute that to I have no idea, but it seems my life has always been that way. I have never been comfortable in windy situations, and I do attribute that to the Santa Ana winds* that brought me into this world.

At about age three, I began my singing career—standing up in church and singing solos like "Jesus Loves Me." I don't think this is

*Mother*
*(Made Dress Herself)*

terribly unusual, but everyone made a big fuss over me and my ability to carry a tune at that young age. Of course, my ability might have had something to do with the fact that my mother was a brilliant pianist and played for us children every night after supper. We did love to hear her play—all the wonderful classics that I was fortunate to hear in my early years: Brahms, Beethoven, Chopin—you name them, I heard them. My mother did not care a lot for Mozart and Bach. She liked much more passionate music. Mother could have been a concert pianist, but in those days, when you married and had children, your job was to stay home and

---

* Called alternately "Santanas," "Santa Anas," and "Devil Winds," they are a phenomenon that occurs in the coastal regions of Southern California during the late fall and winter months.

raise them. So that is what she did. But I always felt there was a great void in her life because she did not use her expertise and love of the piano for her soul's satisfaction.

My dad and uncle had better-than-average tenor voices, so I believe I came by some of my talent genetically. I was blessed with perfect pitch which even my mother did not possess. So I got a lot of attention for my musical abilities and, looking back, I imagine I was a pretty precocious child.

*Father*

When I was five years of age, we had a family tragedy that changed our lives forever. My younger brother, Bobby, became what today is termed "developmentally disabled," but what in those days was simply known as "retarded." He had survived a bad virus (no antibiotics then), and parts of his brain were literally burned out from the high fevers and convulsions. It was a terrible blow to our family. I certainly did not continue to receive the attention I had been used to, and by the time I was seven or eight years old, I was an unhappy and difficult child to deal with.

*Marge & Tom*

However, my grandparents lived next door to us, and they spoiled me a lot. I really could do no wrong. As I have looked back on it, my older brother, Tom, was supposed to be the little man and do chores and not complain. I, on the other hand, did not have to do much except sing and practice a little piano. That instrument I had no patience for, and having my mother as my teacher was probably not the best idea in the world. But since she was so good, why pay to have someone

3

else teach me? Besides, it was during some pretty lean years financially for our family—the Depression.

At about age twelve, I began elocution lessons. I believe we called them that in those days. Probably no one uses that word today. My teacher's name was Mrs. Schaeffer and she lived across the street from us. Don't ask me what her background was, but my folks thought she had something to offer me with these lessons. What I learned was all kinds of speech intonations, lots of diction, and actually speaking words to music—way before the time it became a popular way of sprechtstimme (speaking like Rex Harrison did in *My Fair Lady* and like Richard Burton did in *Camelot*).

I didn't know how advanced I was. To this day I still have some of the pieces and poems that were set to music that I practiced as speech exercises. It was a wonderful way of expressing myself at a young age and certainly did not harm the voice. There was a natural projection of the sound when you spoke in rhythm on top of the music.

By the time I was in high school, the population of Santa Ana was about twenty thousand. My singing and acting continued to develop, and I certainly did get to sing a lot in that small town. Because I had a big voice and quite a range, there was plenty of solo work for me both in church and at school. We had one auditorium—the high school auditorium—and I sang and also acted there many times.

*High School Play*
*(Marge on far left, black dress with square neckline)*

About that time, my parents decided I should have more formal singing training, so I started going to a teacher in Glendale, California. Every Saturday morning, the soprano soloist from our church took me with her to Glendale, about an hour's drive, and we both had our singing lessons. Of course, I felt extremely grown up to be in the Los Angeles area where all the "big stuff" was happening. At least it looked like that to a sixteen-year-old. So, I continued to be the vocal queen in high school and in the area where I lived. And this is how I got attention, because I never felt very attractive or pretty. (I'm sure that sounds familiar to a few of you reading this book.)

After high school it was time to think about my college education. My greatest desire was to go to Occidental College, near Los Angeles, but as the time grew near, I was told that the campus housing was full and I would be living off-campus. (This was September of 1945 and all the men were returning from World War II and getting into college on the G.I. Bill. Campuses were getting very full again and it was a wonderful and exciting time for us young girls.)

The idea of not living on campus did not sound like much fun to me, so my folks contacted the president of Muskingum College in New Concord, Ohio. My parents had gone there, my mother had taught piano there, my grandfather, I believe, had taught there, and some distant cousins had gone there. In other words, there was a lot of family history connected to that small United Presbyterian College. (Many of you will know of this college and New Concord, Ohio, because that is where the astronaut John Glenn and his wife Annie came from.)

I also thought that it might be fun to go East and be in the snow and cold weather. I enjoyed it immensely and had such a good time there. However, I did not agree with the teaching methods of the head of the vocal department (after all, I was almost eighteen years of age and knew all there was to know about singing). At the time, I felt he would be destructive for my voice, and in that assumption I believe I was correct.

So, I switched from a voice major to a piano major which, at the time, I thought was one of the most horrendous decisions of my life. I did not have a great deal of proficiency at the piano, but I certainly had the musical background for it and a little aptitude. I probably did not work hard enough on my lessons, but that's because I found a lot of other interests at college, including boyfriends.

♪

In retrospect, my decision to become a piano major turned out to be one of my better life decisions. It really came in handy for learning opera and musical theater roles for myself and teaching other people their music. Little did I know then how important it would be for me in later years to be able to play the piano for my own voice students.

The good part was that the two piano teachers, the Schnitkers (husband and wife), were absolutely terrific people and good musicians. How that small college ever got them to teach there I will never know. And not only teach there, but stay there for their entire teaching careers! They were both great role models for us young musicians. To this day, we are still in touch with each other and love to talk, talk, talk when we get together at reunions.

There were a lot of strict rules at Muskingum, but we managed to get around many of them. And it was fun to break the rules. (I feel that it is a shame today that there are so few rules to be broken.) There was no smoking on campus, and drinking was strictly out at any time. The drinking was not a problem, but a lot of us had started smoking early in life, so we had to sneak around with that problem. Also, there were definite curfew times. But it seemed there was always someone to let us back in through a window or a door.

By my second year at Muskingum, I was engaged to a fellow student who was what we called a "town boy." It was great to go with a town boy because you always had a home to go to and cooked meals. It was fun to have a feeling of a place to go to get away from the dorm. But that engagement did not last terribly long because I wanted to get on with my life and singing career.

One thing that happened in my second year was one of my sorority sisters knew how much I wanted to see New York City and attend a performance at the Metropolitan Opera House. So at Easter break in 1947, she invited me to go to her home on Staten Island. I had another college friend, Pat Hill, who was going to Long Island for Easter break. She wanted to go to the Met too. I wrote the Met and asked for two tickets to be saved for me for a production of *The Barber of Seville* on a given night.

Marge and Bob Given
(my "town boy")

None of our other friends were interested in that idea, so I was told how to take the Staten Island ferry to lower Manhattan and then take the subway to 42nd Street. Then it was only a short walk to 39th Street where the Met was located in those days. Pat came in on the Long Island Railroad, and we met at the box office of the Met.

I went up to the box office and asked for my tickets. I had the money to pay for them, in cash, of course. Imagine my eighteen-year-old surprised self when there were no reserved tickets for me. I stood there crying in front of the box office attendant and explained my whole story. What a bore for a New York person. But I wouldn't give up. She kept saying that there were no seats left for that performance.

Finally she relented and told us to go down the street to the drugstore and ask for "Joe." Being so naïve, I knew nothing about "scalpers," so off we went. Asked for "Joe" and he came out from the back. I explained in all innocence what had happened, and he said he had two tickets in the balcony for that night's performance. Then he told us how much the tickets would cost! Guess what? I started to cry again, sobbing that we did not have that much money with us. He looked so disgusted with these two kids and grumbled away until finally he said, "Well, how much money do you have?" We told him and he just sighed, shook his head, and gave us the tickets. I was so thrilled when we went into the Opera House. My eyes were bugging out of my face at everything I saw.

The finish to this episode is that the seats were behind a post, but I didn't care. I was hooked. However, when I was told later that there was more than one subway line in New York City, I almost fainted. I had simply taken the first train that came along, and it just "happened" to be the right one. God had looked after both Pat and me that night.

♪

My introduction to New York City!!!!!

I stayed at Muskingum for only two years because I felt that I was not getting enough of what I wanted: more performing skills, more music, and more opportunities to sing. When I found out that in order to graduate from Muskingum I had to take biology, I went to the dean and said I couldn't take that course. He said that I had to in order to graduate. I went to the president, talked with him, and got the same answer. So there was no way around it. It may seem silly to you, but I could not sit in a laboratory and dissect a frog or any of that stuff—so I didn't. It probably was only an excuse not to go back to college, but I didn't see it that way at the time.

I thought about transferring my credits to Occidental, but when I learned that I would lose so many credits and have to repeat courses, I simply made the announcement to my family that I did not want to return to any college. "Wow." That was a big disappointment to my parents and other family members. But they did survive it and did help me get on with my studies and my career.

# ♪ Chapter Two ♫

## Beginning My Singing Career

*"Imagination is the beginning of creation.*
*You imagine what you desire,*
*You will what you imagine*
*and at last you create what you will"*
*~George Bernard Shaw*

♪

Imoved to Glendale, California, to continue my voice and acting
lessons. There were some outlets for performing in that area, so close
to Los Angeles, and when I was only nineteen I got a really great
break. Or so I thought.

This big break was being asked to perform the role of Carmen in
the opera *Carmen* by Bizet. The production was to be directed by Rico
Marcelli. He had a dream to start a Los Angeles opera company, and this
was the first opera he wanted to perform. It was 1949 and there was an
organization in Los Angeles called The Opera Workshop. It was funded by
the G.I. Bill for eligible singers who wanted to make a career in opera. Of
course, they needed some women to play the scenes with them, and I had
joined that group.

The only professional opera I had seen growing up in Southern
California was the San Francisco Opera when it came to Los Angeles and
played a short season at the Shrine Auditorium. But I loved it and went to
see those operas every season from the time I was about thirteen. My poor
parents would take me to L.A. and sit through Wagnerian operas, which
were very, very long. It never bothered me to sit through them, because I
loved the sound of Wagner's music.

My favorite Wagnerian soprano was Helen Traubel. What a voice
she had! Also, the heldentenor Lauritz Melchior. That was some singing,
and I loved to hear it live in a big barn like the Shrine Auditorium.
Probably not ideal for singers, but I didn't know the difference, and their
voices rang out so true and strong that my ears were filled with the beauty
of their singing.

Well, I had a fantastic experience learning the role of Carmen and
working on it with an older woman who had done the role in Europe. Her
name was Mme. Marguerite Sylva. She was an imposing woman, and I
was in total awe of her. But she was kind and wonderful to this raw kid
who certainly did not have the life experience to play Carmen. I learned so
much from her about the character and the acting of Carmen. One thing I
have never forgotten was when she told me that Carmen was not *immoral*,
but *amoral*. A big difference in how I would play her. I loved the singing

*Mme. Marguerite Sylva*

and I think I was pretty good in the role—at least the reviewers thought so. However, no opera company was formed because no one would support it financially, including the city of Los Angeles.

I was still studying voice and acting in Glendale, and it was there that I met and married my husband, Bill Rivingston. We both studied with the same voice teacher, Joe Klein, and he had a large room on the back of his studio where all his students were able to rehearse and perform the arias they were working on. This was a wonderful way to get up in front of your peers and try out your audition pieces. We were all doing a lot of classical concert work at that time.

So, how to make a living singing? Sounds familiar, doesn't it? Some things never change. Well, I sang in churches and women's clubs

*Marge & Bill*

and put together a show of Broadway musical tunes with Bill, who had a beautiful baritone voice. We thought we would make a good duo team. The duo turned into a trio act with our good friend Iona Noble. To save paying a pianist, I accompanied and sang on our gigs.

We were good. We were so good that the Rodgers and Hammerstein office found out what we were doing (without paying royalties to them) and we

♪

*Marge, Bill & Iona*

were stopped. Too bad, because we were making money, and it was great training. So that was the first time my piano work came in handy. (It seems to keep cropping up as my career goes on.)

# ♪ Chapter Three ♬

## New York, Here We Come

*"Whoever uses the spirit that is in him*
*creatively is an artist...*
*To make a living itself and art, that is the goal"*
*~Henry Miller*

♪

About this time, my itch to go to New York City began to really get to me. I was ready to get out of Los Angeles. So in 1952, my husband and I drove our ancient Oldsmobile all the way to the Big Apple. Was I scared? Yes, I was. It was traumatic, but exhilarating. Luckily we had friends there who took us under their wing and helped us find a small apartment. (I strongly recommend that you know someone in that big city before embarking on that journey.)

We arrived in the city on July 4, 1952. What a time to drive into New York City! It was a madhouse and we were so-o-o lost. Knowing now how easy it really is to find your way around the city, I am astounded that we had so much trouble finding West 75th Street and Riverside Drive. If you can find your way around Los Angeles, New York is a breeze.

Well, we finally found our friends and started to move into our apartment. I went out to buy some essentials at Woolworths, which in those days was at 79th Street and Broadway. Not very far away. Well, I went about two blocks and had to return to the apartment, I was so scared. Garbage cans lining the streets, a lot of noise, cars, and buses, and I swear I didn't hear anyone speaking English. My husband had to go out with me to the store. After about two weeks, I was fine and the city seemed more friendly to me. (So don't ever feel embarrassed when you first arrive there and feel less than secure.)

Now it was time to figure out how we were going to make a living there with our talents. I got a part-time job. Bill had already contracted to sing for Dr. Raymond Charles Barker at his church, the Church of Religious Science, which met at Town Hall on Sunday mornings. That was a real blessing—in more ways than one. We found tremendous support at the church, both for ourselves and for our talents. Eventually, I sang there too as part of a quartet, and we were paying our bills.

We were fortunate to be living downstairs from a gentleman who was one of the house managers at the Metropolitan Opera House, so we were able to get standing room and seats for many operas—free. This was when we were both dreaming of being opera stars. But when I saw my first musical—*Bells Are Ringing* with Judy Holliday—that did it for me. It changed my whole musical picture. I thought of all the struggle connected with opera, and I had already faced the fact that I did not think I had the superb vocal talent that it would take to become a successful opera singer. So I fell in love with the musical theater and it has remained my love throughout my life as a performer and as a teacher.

My husband's operatic career did not take off as we had planned it would. By this time, I was making the living for both of us and that began to take its toll on me. I was working during the day and singing in churches on the weekends, so it was a pretty busy life. One fun thing we did was to be on *Arthur Godfrey's Talent Scouts*, which was a television talent show. Bill won it. He had a gorgeous voice, and he got paid to be on the show every day for a week. On the first day, I got to sit with Arthur and discuss our careers. That money really helped, but it didn't seem to generate the kind of interest we thought it would. In addition, I was getting sick a lot, and things began to be difficult between us. There were differences that we were not able to resolve. I was ambitious to be successful in NYC, but Bill did not have the same drive. A pretty unhappy time. But I had learned to love New York and knew I wanted to stay there forever.

I always tell everyone who will listen that New York is a tough town and doesn't care very much about your life or your happiness. You have to live by its terms. Truth becomes very apparent. If you have issues you have not been willing to look at in your life, New York will force you to look into your heart and mind.

Ultimately, the next thing to happen was separation and divorce. Not a pleasant thing for anyone to go through. But I learned how to live alone for the first time and I learned how to appreciate myself and move on in my own development. That is the most courageous thing that anyone can do, both as a person and as an artist. So out I went on my own.

# ♪ Chapter Four ♫

## My Performing Career

*"Life is a song - sing it,*
*Life is a game - play it,*
*Life is a challenge - meet it,*
*Life is a dream - realize it,*
*Life is a sacrifice - offer it,*
*Life is love - enjoy it"*
*~Sai Baba*

♪

*Long-Hair Glamour*

I t wasn't too long until I made my move into the theater that I loved so much. First job—the chorus of summer stock in Rye, New York. Ten weeks, ten different shows. So you move fast, and how I appreciated the fact that I could read music proficiently and learn quickly. However, there is one problem that can show up from being able to read and learn quickly: Every musical director in the world will want to keep you in the chorus because it makes his job so much easier. Not only can you learn your own music, but you can also teach everyone else the music. You will never want for a job, but it is not the way to get ahead in your career. Sometimes, you have to say "No, I want to do a part. I am not doing chorus anymore." (Now, that does not always apply to a Broadway show if you really need the money.) Same thing applies to understudying all the time. When is it your turn to get to do the part? It is hard to say no, but it is the way to get people to listen to you.

It was interesting to me that during that first season of summer stock, I hung out mostly with the dancers in the company. I learned very early that singers only thought from the neck up and were not a lot of fun to be with. Dancers worked as a team and thought about each other and also exercised, which I found to be a good thing. So I had a ball that summer and wanted to do more of the same.

*Sexy Marge*

I took the train to West Palm Beach, Florida, and did one more stock chorus job. Actually, what I remember about that season was how nice it was to be in Florida in the wintertime and not in New York sloshing around. But after that job, I said to my agents, "No more chorus jobs. I'll wait until I land a part." They were not happy to hear that, as they did make money handling me, but I stuck to my guns, changed agents, and went with a wonderful man by

Ado Annie in Oklahoma

Bonnie Le Tour in Anything Goes
with Andy Devine & Bill Hayes

Cleo in
Most
Happy Fella

Meg in Brigadoon

the name of Henry Weiss.

I did get to do parts and I loved it. I was basically the comic relief in most of the shows that I did. Some of my favorites were Ado Annie in *Oklahoma*, Meg in *Brigadoon*, Cleo in *Most Happy Fella* (one of my all-time favorites), Gloria in *Damn Yankees*,

Lizzie in 110 in the Shade

♪

Walking Happy

Clementina (the red-headed Spanish lady) in *The Desert Song*, and Bonnie LeTour (the gun moll) in *Anything Goes*. All of these were stock jobs in various theaters around the country.

*The Desert Song* was produced at the St. Louis Municipal Opera and it was a huge outdoor venue. You could not see the audience from the stage, and finding your way on and off the stage was a challenge. The sets were full-size houses and the backdrops spectacular. Julie Wilson was the star of *Anything Goes*. I played the gun moll and understudied Julie. Not that I ever had a chance to do the part. Julie was such a pro and still is. On one matinee day, Julie and I were going to have dinner together between shows. She kept stopping to sign autographs and talk with people, and I just got antsy waiting for her. When we got to dinner, she said to me, "You will never be a star because you are not willing to give the time to your public." And she was right!

I did not get to do any leading ladies until later when I got to do Lizzie in *110 in the Shade*. That was my favorite show to sing and act. Then *Walking Happy*—not a well-known show, but it had some success on Broadway. I loved my fellow actors and singers. We became friends and those friendships have lasted.

During these jobs that I was doing out of NYC, I found that other performers were asking me if I could help them learn their parts for upcoming shows. Since I could play the piano decently—not brilliantly, but decently—I would say sure. We would then find a piano someplace that wasn't being used and spend an afternoon or day off working on musical comedy scores. It was a wonderful education for me because I was learning all these musicals and the individual parts. Both male and female. I see now that all of this was pointing in the direction of my becoming a teacher.

I also had a big mouth (remember my howling birth) and didn't have any trouble telling people that I thought some phrase or vowel would sound better if they tried it my way or another way. It worked. That gave me some confidence in the fact that I could hear things, change them, and make a song sound better. I was able to make a singer feel more comfortable with the material they were learning and more confident in the way they used their voice in the material.

# ♪ Chapter Five ♫

## Moving to Florida and Back

*"Man is asked to make of himself
what he is supposed to become
to perfect his destiny"*
~Paul Tillich

♪

Now it was time to screw up my life and try another marriage. This man lived in Florida and I had met him in 1959 while I was doing summer stock down there. The reason behind this running away to Florida was that I had been in a long relationship with a married man in New York. Bad choice if you want to have a future with someone (more about this later in the book). But going along chronologically, I chose to get married and move away from New York and the relationship. I believe I had that well-known feminine urge to have children, and I was getting into my thirties and time was running out.

I did work some in Florida and mainly had a nice house and a nice life. However, it was not *my* life! I was so homesick for my friends in New York and for my life in New York and the theater. "A nice man, a nice house, and my heart was not there." So, four years later I divorced and headed back to the Big Apple. No children, so that was a blessing.

Now I was a few years older (hopefully wiser) and work was not that easy to come by. I still had my wonderful agent and he tried to put me up for any show he thought I would be right for. Again, how to make a living in NYC. To help with that, I started teaching piano to children on the West Side. That and singing in churches and temples made me a decent living. In order to get more work, I also sang with some rather famous choral groups. Here again, because I could read music quickly and was an alto, I got these choral jobs pretty easily.

The main group I sang with was The Camerata Singers. I had a friend, Carolyn Friday, who was singing with them, and she got me the audition. I passed. We sang a lot of oratorio, cantatas, Beethoven's *Ninth Symphony*, Mahler, and more than I can remember. It was quite an experience to be sitting in Avery Fisher Hall with the likes of Leonard Bernstein conducting the New York Philharmonic Orchestra. Tommy Schippers and Lucas Foss were hot conductors at that time also. Some others I can't remember, but one would never forget singing with Leonard Bernstein. What an incredible ear that man had. He could pick out one instrument for either a wrong note or a dynamic level and change the whole sound of the orchestra.

♪

I was entranced sitting up in back of the orchestra and watching him work. He was famous for conducting with a very strong arm motion, and often his baton would end up either in the middle of the orchestra or in the auditorium. He never cared. The music was the only thing that mattered. It was a glorious experience of being with the best and hearing the best during the late 1960s.

I worked with these choral groups for about two years. One performance that we did was when Leonard Bernstein and Lillian Hellman, the composer and lyricist of *Candide*, were looking for a way to produce a revival of the show. We did a concert version with Madeline Kahn as Cunegonde. She was magnificent in the role. Later she came to study with me for a while and I told her how impressed I had been with her singing of Cunegonde. This was her remark to me: "Oh, I can't really sing that high, so I just let the character do it and then I could make the notes. But I couldn't ever sing those notes myself." Interesting "take" on releasing fear through the character.

Then at a lesson one day, she told me that she couldn't study with me anymore. I was shocked and asked her why. Her answer was that her mother had been an opera singer (which I did not know). She never felt that she measured up in any way to her mother's talent. (I believe she thought she might measure up and that was something she wasn't prepared for with her mother.) She also said that I made singing too easy and that it should be hard. Oh my, what a loss that was for me.

By that time, I was also back with my lover Carl, "The Married Man" of years before, and my decision was to stay in New York and live my life the way I wanted to and with the person I wanted to be with. It was not an easy decision to make in the '60s—not at my age and with my upbringing. But I had always been an independent thinker and so I did it "my way."

Then in 1972, I got the opportunity to do Lady Thiang in *The King and I* in San Diego. What a great time we all had. The show was in conjunction with the Performing Arts School there, and a few of us were Equity professionals brought in on a Guest Artist contract. It was

♪

a wonderful production with Shani Wallace and William Chapman. I loved singing the music that Lady Thiang sang. The song "Something Wonderful" is truly almost an aria and so singable. We were performing

Shani Wallace, Marge, Chula Longhorn, William Chapman in The King & I

outdoors in the park, and there were seals and other animals in the neighboring zoo you could hear while the show was going on. We took it all in stride and it was a magical time.

One night as I was in the scene where Lady Thiang tries to get Mrs. Anna to go to the King, I completely lost my lines. I stood there facing Shani, and she just stared back at me. It was probably no more than thirty seconds, but it was an eternity before I could think of something to say. I think I wandered or rambled a bit and finally got back on cue. After the show, Shani apologized to me for not being able to help with my lines, but she didn't know them. Sometimes you do know other people's lines and can give them a clue, but in this case I was out there on my own. I'm sure the audience didn't even know what had happened, but it sure makes you panic for that moment.

I also did the part of the Mother Abbess in *The Sound of Music* in Flint, Michigan, with Carol Lawrence. Now let me tell you that when you do that part, you live like a nun during the run. "Climb Every Mountain" is as difficult to sing as any aria I know. And you are performing it eight times a week. You never would do that in the opera world.

# ♪ Chapter Six ♫

## Opera Fun

*"She is a singer and therefore capable of anything"*
*~Vincenzo Bellini - (1801-1835) Italian Opera Composer*

♪

During the next few years, I did sing some opera with the New York City Opera Educational Program that was headed by my friend and mentor Thomas Martin—the same man who had given me my second paying job in the business. Thomas had hired me for a season of summer stock in Skaneateles, New York, in the days of performing in tents. Skaneateles is one of the beautiful Finger Lakes of central New York State.

It was a concert tour called *An Evening with Johann Strauss.* Our soprano soloist was none other than Miss Beverly Sills. She had not yet become the big opera diva, but all the talent and voice were there.

An Evening with Johann Strauss Tour
Marge 2nd from left - Beverly Sills 2nd from right

One thing about Beverly Sills was that she never needed to warm up her voice very much before a performance. She would simply come in the room, do about two scales up and down and say, "Okay, I'm all warmed up." The rest of us would be singing for twenty minutes, and now I realize that she was the smart one: over-warming up can take the beautiful bloom off the voice and have it appear to be a little tired when you are performing. Each individual really has to know their own instrument and how long it takes to warm it up but not wear it out. There is a saying "don't leave your performance in the dressing room!" So too much warming up is not good for your performance. Beverly was fun to be with, and the whole group was quite compatible.

♪

Johann Strauss did not write much for the alto or mezzo voice, but what little there was, I got to do as the alto soloist. That was a thrill for me at that time. We were on the road for ten weeks. And because we were singing Viennese waltzes, the costumes were dresses with big hoop skirts and dyed-to-match shoes. It was truly horrendous to deal with those costumes. Getting on and off the bus with them was clumsy at best, and when it rained—well, you can imagine. We always dressed at the hotels as there usually were no dressing rooms at the auditorium or gym where we were performing. It was winter, so that created another hazard with dresses and shoes. There were thirteen of us and two pianos. We traveled by bus and there was no bathroom on that bus (much easier today). So we had to stop every few hours to get off the bus and get something to eat and drink and use the facilities.

One time when we were traveling through the South, we stopped for our usual reasons, and when we all got back on the bus, it took us about ten or fifteen miles to realize we had left Max, one of the pianists, back at the pit stop. What an uproar. Thomas Martin was Viennese and had a temperament that blew up rather readily. He was furious. We were all concerned about Max, but Thomas was angry just thinking he had to turn the bus around and go back for Max.

Actually we stopped and called back and found out that Max had called a taxi to meet us down the road. So we waited. He arrived and was pretty upset with all of us that we had not checked to see that everyone was back on the bus before we left. Let me tell you—that never happened again. We counted noses so-o-o many times.

Some of the auditoriums we played were really gymnasiums. We were in some small towns that did not have their own auditoriums or theaters. Again, it was a terrific experience, but I pretty much decided right then that I did not like what is called a "bus and truck tour." Which means that you were moving almost every day and spending so many hours in the bus. That tour lasted ten weeks, and in that length of time you really got to know the people you were traveling with. Sometimes fun, sometimes not.

Back to the City Opera days. I did *The Old Maid and the Thief* by Menotti and played the part of Miss Todd. I loved playing an older spinster lady who was extremely proper and stiff. We did another opera, *The Consul*, which was wonderful singing (containing some beautiful melodies). We performed these operas for schools, and it was a good introduction to opera for young people. The operas were in English anyway, so that was a plus for students of all ages.

Four of us decided that we could do the same thing with the schools and make more money for ourselves, so we started our own small opera company. The opera that we did the most and that was the most successful was Seymour Barab's *Little Red Riding Hood*. It was so cleverly written and a real pleasure to sing. We did all our own costumes and sets, and I played the part of the Grandmother.

Again, I loved doing the character

Marge & Joyce Hall

part and have always felt that those parts were more fun to play than most leading-lady roles. You get to portray someone totally unlike yourself (or so you think). The children loved the Wolf and Little Red. My hair was tied up in a knot on the top of my head and I looked pretty awful. So when we would meet the children

Joyce, Marshall & Marge

afterwards to talk with them, I would put a wig on so I didn't look so severe and scare the little kids.

We often did morning and afternoon performances, so we had to find a place to have lunch between shows. Most of the time we all had something light to eat and coffee to drink. However, once in a while we would splurge and have a glass of wine with our lunch. For me, that was not a good idea because I tended to forget my lyrics if I had anything alcoholic to drink.

So one day between performances at one of the schools, I had a glass of wine with lunch and I literally forgot where I was in the show and mixed up some lyrics. A terrible performance, but we got through it. The rest of the cast were laughing onstage at me, but the kids in the audience really did not know that anything was wrong. After that show, however, I was told by my peers that I was never allowed to have wine with lunch again. I truly agreed with them. We did these operas for a couple of years and then we all got so busy with other projects (me with teaching) that we decided to disband the company.

# ♪ Chapter Seven ♫

## Bette Midler

*"Nourish your inner light*
*then trust it to illuminate your path"*
*~Bernard Rands, Musician-Composer*

♪

I was beginning to teach a lot at that time, and in 1978 I received a call from my old voice teacher in California telling me that she had been coaching and teaching Bette Midler. And now Bette was in New York and looking for someone to study singing with, and I had been suggested by Esther Andreas. (Esther was a wonderful opera teacher in Los Angeles and also came to New York City for the City Opera each season. She had many students in the company and would come and stay in the city for about four months each year. So I had the privilege of always being able to study with her in California and New York.)

Well, that was a shock. The first thing I did was to call my friend David Friedman and ask him if *he* knew Bette Midler. Of course he did, but I only knew her name and had never heard her sing. David suggested I run out pronto and buy a record of hers, and so I did—immediately!

I had never worked with that type of singing and I was a little nervous about how to approach Bette and her singing technique. She was in New York doing *Divine Madness* on Broadway. She came over and turned out to be a very willing student. She wanted to learn whatever she could about singing technique and how to improve her singing abilities. That made it easier for me to explain some basic things to keep her voice healthy throughout the run of the show. Also, knowing that she had loved working with Esther, I felt I had something to offer her.

Of course, she was doing eight performances a week and that really takes its toll on the voice. Particularly the high-energy performance that Bette always gives. I remember saying to her at one time or another, "What is the use in being a star if you still have to do all the work? Let some of the other performers do some numbers and you take more time off during the show." No way! Bette would never cheat her audience of one minute of her time. She is such a hard worker and always expects everyone around her to work as hard as she does.

One of my favorite stories during that time was that quite often her lesson would be before or after Sarah Jessica Parker's. I believe Sarah Jessica was about thirteen or fourteen at the time and doing the part of Annie in *Annie* on Broadway. Bette was so nice to Sarah Jessica and, of course, Sarah Jessica was in total awe of Bette.

One day at the end of Sarah Jessica's lesson, she said to me that she wanted to see Bette's show. *Annie* was dark on Monday night and Bette's show had a Monday night performance. Well, that did not work out. When I asked Bette about tickets for Sarah Jessica and her mother or me to take her, Bette said, "No way is that child going to see my show." I was really surprised. The show, of course, was a little raunchy and I had not seen it yet, so I really didn't know quite how raunchy it was. I said that Sarah Jessica had grown up in the theater and show business and there wasn't a lot that she would be shocked by, but Bette still said "no way."

Sarah Jessica was so disappointed, but I thought how sweet it was that Bette did not want her to see the show and hear all the language in it. Since that time, Bette and Sarah Jessica have done movies together and are friends. A funny and marvelous world, the world of show business.

Speaking of that element of the business, it occurs to me to say that one of the reasons I have always loved show people is that they are so honest in their feelings and that they spend their life trying to understand themselves. I respect show people because they don't hide the real person within. In order to be a good actor, actress, singer or dancer, they must explore their own emotions and bring them to the surface. No hiding. A big job to be sure.

And people who think that show business is simply having fun have never been around the theater. Or a movie set or a recording studio. What a hard and demanding job it all is. The work is so intense and the rejection level so high that one must have a tremendous amount of tenacity and feeling of self-worth or self-esteem to "hang in there." The glamour part is the smallest component of the life you have to lead. Then, when you have so-called "arrived," the next job is how to stay on top. And at the same time, trying to maintain a life outside the theater—husband, wife, children—whatever one needs to keep sane.

In 1979, right after Bette finished *Divine Madness*, she was getting ready to make the movie *The Rose*. What a fantastic opportunity that was for her. Well, I happened to be visiting my parents in California, about sixty miles south of Los Angeles, at the time when she was making the sound track for the movie. What a hard job that was. So taxing on the voice. I would drive up to her house in Beverly Hills in the morning and she would literally have no voice left from the recording session the day before. We would start easy and light to even get a singing sound started, and then coax it along for an hour or more, and finally her voice would start to respond. That taught me how resilient the vocal apparatus really is. It was very slow, careful work, but it sure paid off. I truly believe that movie started Bette's career in another direction altogether. I lost track of her for many years as she became the movie star. And she is great at that too. I caught up with her later.

# ♪ Chapter Eight ♫

## Teaching Broadway Singers

*"Music is the divine way*
*to tell beautiful, poetic things to the heart"*
*~Pablo Casals*

♪

Back to the story of my involvement in the theater. In 1973, Broadway did a revival of *Irene* with Debbie Reynolds. My niece Penny Worth had just gotten into the chorus of the show. About six of the chorus members came to study with me. Eight shows a week was a pretty demanding job for a singer. I began to change my ideas of how to teach singing.

The idea, it seemed to me, was to keep the voice healthy and strong for a long run, possibly a year or more. Here you are, doing the same music, the same range, the same words, show after show. The repetition becomes tiring for the voice. Try singing a hymn with five or six verses and see what your voice feels like when you are finished. For most singers, it is one of the most tiring exercises on the voice.

So I started thinking that how you warmed up your voice at the beginning of the week was not necessarily the way you would warm it up by the end of the week. Or by the seventh or eighth show. You must give the voice variety. So, if you are doing a belting role (not my favorite way to have to use the voice), you must warm up more in the head voice. That helps to balance the singing you are doing in the show eight times a week.

In 1979, I got a call from one of my students, Alix Korey. The musical director of *Ain't Misbehavin'* had called her to help the singers who were going into the road company of that show. Alix did not profess to be a voice teacher, although she knew a lot about the voice and vocal technique. However, Bill Elliott, the musical director, had worked with her on a show and "thought she knew everything" about singing. Alix told Bill to call me, but he panicked and said "no voice teachers." Maybe he had had a bad experience with a voice teacher at some time or another and was afraid I would tamper with the singers' style that was necessary for this production.

It was mostly a revue type of show with staging, and there were twenty-six numbers in the show; only four people in the cast. Each one had a lot of singing to do and to learn. So, Alix would call me at night and ask me questions that she had about what a singer was doing or having trouble with, and I would make some suggestions. Then she would go in the next day and try to put the ideas to use with the singers. Well, after a couple of weeks of this, Alix got a job that was going to take her out of town. Again, she told Bill Elliott to call me and that I was perfectly safe to have around his singers. I wasn't going to change their entire way of singing or confuse them with too much technique talk. So Bill finally called me, and I went in and met all the singers and the director, Richard Maltby.

The job was challenging because the singing was so difficult to maintain show after show. The cast was wonderful and accepted the help I was able to give them. Mainly it was about how to keep their voices healthy while doing a long run on the road. One of those "tricks," as I call them, is to "warm down" after a hard-singing show. In the shower or at home before going to bed, take five to seven minutes to get the muscles in the throat relaxed and in their proper mode before going to sleep. I found that leaving the muscles in the state they are in after the show tends to keep the tension in the muscles all night long. This I do believe was a great help and continues to be a great help to anyone who will take the time and make the effort to "warm down" when they are performing a difficult show eight times a week—either on the road or in a Broadway show. This also goes for actors in difficult and wordy plays and parallels the "cooling down" period for dancers. This "warm down" will be explained more in the exercise section.

Working beside Bill, Richard, and conductor Linda Twine was a great thrill for me. I went to the theater almost every night for a few weeks to see how things were working for the performers. What they do onstage and what they do in a one-on-one voice lesson are two entirely different things. So I learned to always try to attend performances that my students were doing, so that I could gear what I was teaching them to what they were doing with a role onstage. I made some new friends that were pretty high up in the Broadway scene. Of course, that also included the producer who had to pay me.

# ♪ Chapter Nine ♫

## The Pirates of Penzance:
## The Broadway Company

*"Fly like a bird, take to the sky,*
*I need you now Lord - carry me high!"*
*~Mariah Carey*

♪

Rex Smith, Linda Ronstadt
& Kevin Kline

In 1980, Joe Papp was putting together a production of *The Pirates of Penzance*, which was to be included in the New York Shakespeare Festival's free summer shows in Central Park. Joe managed to gather together a superb cast: Linda Ronstadt as Mabel, Kevin Kline as The Pirate King, Rex Smith as Frederic, George Rose (God rest his wonderful soul and wit) as the Major General, and Patricia Rutledge from London as Ruth. Also the most stunning-sounding Broadway chorus you can imagine.

The way that I happened on the scene was that I received a call that Linda was having some trouble singing "Poor Wand'ring One." Now, that was her main song, almost like a coloratura aria. Linda had never really tried to bridge her voices together—the bottom and the extraordinary top—and she didn't know how to accomplish this vocally. She was really scared that it was not coming out well, so when Bill Elliott suggested that I might help her with the number, she agreed right away to have me come down to the Public Theater so she could sing "Poor Wand'ring One" for me. That was my introduction to Joe Papp and the rest of the crew at the New York Shakespeare Festival.

I knew immediately what needed to be done to get her chest and head voices to blend together, but—and it was a big "but"—we had so little time to get the job done. However, because Linda has both a fabulous ear and the fantastic ability to initiate new sounds in her voice, we accomplished the almost impossible task by the time the show opened in the Park. (But I want to make the point here that Linda did not let her ego or her huge success in another medium, such as "Rock and Roll," keep her from asking and getting the help she needed right then.)

The show was so successful with Bill Elliott's unbelievably great arrangements and orchestrations that Joe decided to move it to Broadway that following fall. Graciela Daniele was the amazing coordinator of the musical numbers and choreography, and Wilfred Leach was the director. As I understood it later, it was Kevin Kline who came up with some of the bizarre ideas for the staging. I think I would believe that. What a talent.

The cast remained intact except for the part of Ruth. That part was taken over by Estelle Parsons. Now, the story goes that when Joe wanted to hire Estelle for the part, he told her that she had to come and work with me on the singing part of the role. She did not like that idea at all. Joe said that she either came to work with me or she did not get the part.

Well, I felt a slight bit of antagonism toward me when she arrived at my door for her first session. But because she was a pianist, a very good musician, and had a good voice to work with, we quickly got down to business. She became not only a longtime student, but also a good friend—and did a fabulous job as Ruth.

Estelle found and still finds great value in doing the vocal exercises in preparation for the many difficult acting roles that she plays. (Her one-woman shows are such tours de force that she needs all the vocal power she can get to maintain them.) *Pirates*, again, was a huge success on Broadway, and the original cast promised to stay on for six months.

I loved when Linda Ronstadt told me that she was going to do all eight shows a week, even though she had been told that her standby, Karla De Vito, would or could do the matinees for her. Linda had not done a Broadway run in her career, so it seemed like a good idea to have her do only six shows a week and let Karla do the two matinee performances. No way. The problem with having a star like Linda was that people came to see *her*. Sometimes a little different audience than you would usually have at a Broadway performance, and when she was out sick or whatever, the people wanted their money back. Linda adored Joe Papp and did not want him to lose money because of her, so she showed up and went on sometimes when she was not really feeling up to par. The "show must go on" became the rule.

Linda's comment to me was, "If George Rose can do eight shows a week, so can I." Now that was not quite the same thing, since George Rose was a seasoned Broadway veteran and was used to a schedule of eight shows a week. However, Linda did it, and it worked out quite well.

A funny story (not so funny at the time) about Linda and Rex. The reviews had just come out and, as I recall, were nothing short of fantastic. All the papers, magazines, and news reports were great for the show and everyone in the cast. So, the evening show after the reviews were out was something I have never experienced in the theater, although I do believe it could and does happen. Bill Elliott was so proud and happy about the reviews for his orchestrations and the orchestra guys that he had drinks for all of them before the show. (Oops! Not a good idea.) Wilfred, the director, and I had been roaming the theater during all the performances before this time because we were too nervous to sit down front in regular seats—just in case something went wrong and we were needed backstage. But that night, we felt so confident after the reviews that we decided we would trust the show, performers and all, and sit down in the orchestra seats.

Linda came out to do "Poor Wand'ring One" and Rex was onstage with her. She heard the awful sounds of that intoxicated orchestra and started to try to sing, but Rex was making faces at her (which the audience could not see, of course). She began to break up and started giggling. Rex didn't stop "acting up," and they both went to pieces and could not sing.

Poor Wilfred and I were horrified. The audience, by that time, did not think this was at all funny, so Wilfred leaped up from his seat, ran through the audience, rushed backstage and told both of them to go back out on the stage, repeat the number, and do it right. We stopped the show while this was happening and then, lo and behold, Linda and Rex came out very apologetically and did the entire number over. They were wonderful and I don't think I ever heard Linda sing the number better.

One other thing of note is that I believe *Pirates* was the first Broadway musical to be totally amplified. Synthesizers and other electronic instruments in the orchestra made it necessary to mike the singers, but because Linda and Rex were both recording artists and had always performed with amplification, we had to make sure everything balanced soundwise between the orchestra pit and the stage.

Kevin Kline, who was used to projecting his voice, be it speaking or singing, created a different approach for the use of his vocal instrument. Same for George Rose. Kevin, with his tremendous stage energy, was blowing out the sound system with his voice and did not balance with everyone else. I realized that what an actor would have to do under these circumstances would be to keep the body energy (particularly as The Pirate King) and not shout with the voice. But that is not an easy trick to accomplish. As a performer, you are used to connecting the body energy of the role and the voice together for your projection. So, I believe this was the first Broadway show that was fully amplified and in which, for the first time, the actors had to balance their physical energy with less vocal projection.

Personally, I hated the amplification. I didn't like people turning their backs on stage or moving upstage and the sound being all the same. I felt that we had lost something in the theater that we would never get back. And I was right. Every musical today is totally amplified, unlike the former days when there were no microphones on stage and the actors had to project their own sound.

I still love to go to a theater where the actors and actresses are using their God-given instruments to produce a variety of sound for us to listen to. But I have reconciled myself to this now-permanent change, and I sit back and enjoy the show.

# ♪ Chapter Ten ♬

## Pirates Continues

*"In acting as in singing, the nuances of the human voice can express the entire range of emotion, from Joy to Grief"*
*~Rosanne Cash, Singer-Songwriter*

♪

As time went on and it was time for replacements in many of the major roles, I was privileged to work with many more quality performers from all types of musical backgrounds, including the wonderful and multitalented Maureen McGovern. It was funny that my initial meeting with Maureen was almost the same experience as I had with Estelle Parsons.

Marge & Maureen

Maureen was so afraid that I, as a voice teacher, would try to change her way of singing or tamper with her instrument that she did not want to have anything to do with me. But Joe Papp insisted, as he always did, and so the day that Maureen arrived for her first lesson, she brought her manager with her. I could feel the icy air around me, and I thought we were not going to get very far with that feeling. I felt that her manager did not care for me and for the fact that Maureen had to work with me or not do the part.

Happily, Maureen realized very quickly that I was not going to try to change the way that she produced her sound. The only thing I was going to try to do was to (1) enhance the beautiful instrument she had, (2) give her, with vocal exercises, more power and fine-tuning, and (3) teach her how to protect her voice through eight shows a week and on into her long career of singing. At this writing, some twenty-five years later, we still work together when the opportunity presents itself.

I would like to mention the importance of maintaining your vocal instrument. Maureen would never think of going onstage to sing without having properly warmed up her instrument. That means that she is always in good vocal condition. Some singers take a three-month break from singing and then expect to pick up a piece of music and sing it perfectly. That doesn't happen. The voice is a set of muscles that need tuning up the same as any other muscles in the body. If you have to take time off from practicing for health or other reasons, you should start back vocalizing very lightly—lots of breath moving—and only work for ten minutes at a time for a couple of weeks. The other thing is that, in my experience, I have found that the diaphragm and breathing apparatus lose a lot of strength when not used consistently, so you are having to build up the breath capacity again *plus* the voice muscles. Also, as one gets older, one should keep these muscles tuned up all the time; otherwise, it takes too long to get the voice back to performance level.

At the time that Maureen came into *Pirates*, we also were replacing the role of Frederic and the role of The Pirate King. Robby Benson took over the role of Frederic, and Treat Williams the role of The Pirate King. I believe Kaye Ballard also came onboard as Ruth at that point. It was a wonderful exchange of talent, and I was lucky to continue my role of working with each replacement as they took over their roles.

Now we had a road company to think about. It was obvious that this rendition of *Pirates* should become a national road company. So the search began for the Los Angeles company, and then most of that company would continue on to become the road company after a limited Los Angeles run.

I was privileged to be a part of the casting group—and what an experience that was. I had never sat behind a casting table before or realized what the casting group went through trying to sort out the hundreds of people who came in to sing. We needed very specific types for this show. It is quite a process and I certainly was not aware of the intricacies that went into casting an entire show. Wilfred Leach, the director, had an uncanny eye and a sense for people who would make up a company and support and get along with each other. Graciela Daniele needed people who could move well. Bill Elliott and I were looking for who could sing the roles and sustain eight shows a week and be interesting. Also involved were Joe Papp's regular casting people from the

Public Theater.

At the end of each day, we voted for who would be called back and who would not. There was one exception to the chorus call. A girl by the name of Caroline Peyton came into the room, got up to sing whatever she sang, and we all jumped up and said, almost in unison, "Will you be in this production?" That does not happen often. But what a good choice we

*Road Company of Pirates*

made that day. One other girl stuck out as someone we all agreed on, and that was Patti Cohenour. She became the understudy for Pam Dawber who was our Mabel in Los Angeles.

So another superb cast emerged: Barry Bostwick as The Pirate King, Andy Gibb as Frederic, the very British Clive Revill as the Major General, Jo Anne Worley as Ruth, and Paxton Whitehead as the Chief of Police. It was wonderful. They were so professional and wanted to do such a good job with their roles that it was a pleasure and joy to work with all of them on the score.

On opening night in Los Angeles, I was driving to the Ahmanson Theater on the Hollywood Freeway at rush hour—about 5:30 p.m. Traffic, traffic, traffic. I'm in the fast lane and I have a blowout. I was so lucky that the man behind me saw what happened and "ran interference" for me by moving over lane by lane so I could get over to the shoulder. I thought, now what do I do? I was due at the theater by 6 p.m. to warm up each person for the opening, and here I was stuck on the freeway.

To make it all the more fun, you should picture what I looked like. Part of my hair was up in curlers. I was wearing slacks and gold high-heeled shoes and was in full make-up. My long dress was lying across the back seat of the car (in those days we still dressed up for opening nights and parties). When the tow truck came, the driver must have wondered what kind of a nut this was out on the road, although not much would surprise anyone in the Hollywood area.

Well, I was only about half an hour late when it was all done and everything got back on track. You have to remember that we did not have cell phones at that time, so I could not let anyone at the theater know what had happened to me. They were all pretty worried and very glad to see me when I walked in. I did have time to warm up anybody who wanted to and then get myself ready for the performance. Of course, it turned out to be terrific, and the reviews were outstanding.

One story about Barry Bostwick. Barry liked to meditate and concentrate before the performance, and Wilfred had a tendency to come around to dressing rooms and give notes just before the show. Well, Barry didn't like that, so he put a notice up on his dressing room door that said no one was to bother him before curtain time—not even the director. I thought that was great. You need that time to be quiet, think through what you want to do out there in performance, and just be by yourself.

# ♪ Chapter Eleven ♫

## Road Company of Pirates

*"Do the thing and you will have the power"*
*~Ralph Waldo Emerson*

♪

As the road company got cast and the Los Angeles company was closing, the roles changed once again. One fun story was that at the beginning of the L.A. run, Pam Dawber was really sick and could not go onstage. Due to lack of rehearsal time, Patti Cohenour was not prepared yet to do a performance and neither was Caroline Peyton. Linda Ronstadt was in Los Angeles and we called her and asked her if she would do the performance that evening. She actually said yes, though having never rehearsed with this company or the orchestra. We got costumes and wigs ready. I warmed her up. She walked through the staging of the show with Wilfred Leach. Then came the announcement to the audience that Pam Dawber would not be doing the show that night. There was this big groan from the house and then the announcer finished by saying that Linda Ronstadt would be performing the role that night. As you can imagine, the house just roared. Linda did a superb performance that night and we were all eternally grateful to her for saving the day.

*Peter Noone, Caroline Peyton & Jim Belushi*

Back to the road company again. Caroline Peyton was cast as Mabel. Patrick Cassidy was cast as Frederic for the San Francisco Company, and then Peter Noone (Herman's Hermits) was cast in Seattle and for the rest of the tour. Jim Belushi was The Pirate King. Jo Anne Worley was still Ruth for San Francisco, and then Marsha Bagwell was cast in Seattle. Clive Revill, and later Leo Leyden, was the Major General. I had contracted with Joe Papp to open each city, and so I would spend four or five days brushing up everybody before opening in a new city. Now, when a show has been running awhile, it happens that the performers tend to "improve" their roles—add their own "business" instead of keeping to the original staging. Well, the job of the director was to come in and say, "Take out all the improvements and get back to the original staging." That became my job because I was the only member of the original production team who showed up to work with the cast.

Jim Belushi was not a singer, but he had great musical instincts and a love for the music. I had to approve the fact that he would be able to sing it. So, here he came to my apartment for his, I guess I would say, "audition." I did think that with some discipline (not a big asset of his at that time) he could do the role. I knew he really wanted to do it, so we began working on the score and I stuck my neck out and told everybody that he could do it—that he had the comedy timing and the flair for the part of The Pirate King.

At that time, Jim smoked a lot, so he would come to my apartment to take his lesson, and he'd hide his pack of cigarettes by the mail chute in the hallway of my apartment building. Like I couldn't smell smoke on him! He was such an honest guy that he finally told me what he was doing, and we did share that small secret. He kept trying to kick the habit and eventually was successful.

Jim is a wonderful stage performer, which I'm sure not everyone realizes, and he could really read an audience and adjust to their mood. One thing he would say is, "Keep the house cool, because people don't laugh when it is too warm. They fall asleep." He was absolutely right. It was also the year that his brother John died (1982) and so we had much in common, as my lover Carl had passed away that year also. It was hard for Jim to perform sometimes because he had idolized his older brother. So together we did some crying and letter exchanges, and he just tried to get through his show each night.

Peter Noone was a terrific Frederic and was so disciplined in his work, the opposite of Jim, and they did tangle over that once in a while. He was careful to warm up before every performance, and his voice held up very well. Then he went to London and took over the part for a while, and then went with the show to Australia. So he had a good run out of *Pirates.* I got to work with him in London, and we have maintained our friendship. We work together vocally when it is possible.

Working with all these personalities really made me aware of how to work with people and how to respect their talents. They were all so different and already had a lot of success in their fields. So, I, as the teacher, had to learn to use everything they already offered and then fit their voices into the roles they were playing. Most of them were not just stage performers, but recording artists and entertainers.

# ♪ Chapter Twelve ♫

## More Broadway Shows

*"The secret of art is that it converts*
*a fiction into a beautiful artistic truth"*
*~Konstantin Stanislavski, Acting Method*

♪

During that same year, I worked on a show called *The Little Prince*, based on the novel by Antoine de Saint Exupery. The star of that show was Michael York. I worked with him because it was a musical, and he had not done much singing. He was a very nice person, and we got along well. Also in that show was Ellen Greene who became a student of mine later on. The conductor was David Friedman, and through the work we did together on that show, David and I became very good friends and worked on other shows together. If you have never heard of the show, it's because the show closed after only four or five performances.

About that time, Alan Menken was putting together *Little Shop of Horrors* for an off-Broadway production. It opened at the Orpheum Theater on July 27, 1982. Ellen Greene was hired to play the leading role of Audrey, and she contacted me about lessons. It was an extremely difficult role vocally—a lot of high belting—and she really needed someone to be there for her when the going got rough. So she insisted that I be her vocal coach.

The producers were not particularly thrilled with having to pay me to be on call for her and for her weekly voice lesson. However, I do believe the producers, Alan Menken and Howard Ashman, came to realize that it paid off for them to have a good, consistent performance from Ellen.

Howard Ashman was a great director and also knew that I was helping his show stay intact vocally. It was a highly stylized vocal production that they wanted and not terribly easy on the voice week after week. The three young girls—Leilani Jones, Jennifer Leigh Warren, and Sheila Kay Davis—also worked with me to keep their harmony in tune. So I was becoming quite busy.

Then the movie of *Pirates* was being discussed and it ended up being produced in London in 1983—with Linda Ronstadt, Kevin Kline, Rex Smith, George Rose, and Angela Lansbury as Ruth. Estelle Parsons was disappointed not to be chosen as Ruth, but the movie people (producers I imagine) wanted Angela Lansbury's name connected with the project.

♪

Again I got to work with all the chorus people and principals in New York. That is because the sound track for the movie was done by our people from the Broadway company. The chorus people were played by actors and actresses from England. And a terrific group they were. Many of them ended up in the London stage company and I worked with them there.

When the sound track was being finished, I was in Seattle with the road company, and I got a call to go to Los Angeles for a day and work with Linda Ronstadt on the high E-flat at the end of "Poor Wand'ring One." She was not happy with the way it sounded on the movie track, so we went in the studio in Los Angeles, she sang the note a few times, and it was perfect. In order to have the sound of a note like that exactly the way you want to hear it played back, you have to be extremely well warmed up for it. It was a little extra side trip for me, and it was my birthday, so we had a good time after we finished working. I don't believe that the movie turned out all that well, but it is available on VHS with all those marvelous singers.

Carl Brown

So after the movie was finished, it was time to hit London with this irreverent version of *Pirates*. Once again, Joe Papp went to bat for me with the London producers. Michael White, the producer, saw no reason for me to be included in his budget, but Joe persisted in getting him to consider bringing me over, as he really believed that I helped to keep his productions running smoothly. Finally, Michael White agreed to hire me for two weeks to work with the British cast. That happened on April 7, and I was so excited that I would have the great opportunity to work with all of the British cast. However, that night (Tuesday), Carl, my friend and companion of twenty-seven years, died from a heart attack. So it was a bittersweet victory.

A few days later, I did get on the airplane to London. I didn't tell anyone except Graciela Daniele, the choreographer, what had happened. I felt it would make people very careful around me if they knew my sorrow, and I simply wanted to do my work. I told Graciela just in case I suddenly broke down and ran out of the rehearsal. Under those circumstances, one never can tell what might occur.

Graciela took care of me in London—so sympathetic and really there for me during the weeks we were rehearsing *Pirates*. She even moved me to a place closer to her and cooked dinners for me. It was very helpful for me in my healing process. Today she is an active director and choreographer. When I am in New York City, we always try to get together for breakfast or just to see each other. Our birthdays are just four days apart, and we always talk with each other between December 4 and December 8.

Of course the D'Oyly Carte Opera Company was aghast at what we had done to Gilbert and Sullivan, but it sure was a lot more fun than the old stuffy versions. More comedy, different orchestra arrangements, more Broadway-type singing. A quote in the London *Daily Express* said, "The D'Oyly Carte Opera Company had to cancel their 1981–82 season when they failed to get their Arts Council grant because performances were too wooden." So we picked up the 1982 season and were a smash hit.

I worked with everyone in the cast, and it was such a happy time for me. The British are so articulate, work so hard, and have been so well-trained that it was wonderful for me to experience working with these artists. My work was scheduled in between other rehearsals with each person privately. This meant that I was working the longest hours of anyone in the company. One on one certainly takes more time than staging one number with a whole group.

The superb cast was Pamela Stephenson as Mabel, Tim Curry as The Pirate King, Annie Ross as Ruth, Michael Praed as Frederic, and George Cole as the Major General. Most of these stars had never sung a big role before, and some of them had not sung at all. Tim Curry had sung a lot but wanted to really work vocally on The Pirate King. What a nice man he is and such a dynamic and interesting performer. Graciela and I both fell in love with him.

Annie Ross, of course, was a great jazz singer with Lambert, Hendricks and Ross, a famous jazz trio. The trio became an international success, recording and working all over the world. But a book show was not something she had done very often, so that required a different kind of approach vocally. Pamela Stephenson, a great comedienne and actress, had not sung anything like Mabel. It's almost a coloratura soprano part and so that ended up to be a big challenge for her and for me. But she was an excellent Mabel and sang the part very well.

Then there was George Cole. A very famous and renowned actor of stage, movies, and television—who had never sung. Well, the two of us had a marvelous time getting him to do his vocal exercises every day and to get to feel comfortable singing onstage. To this day I am friends with all of them, and they are not only great performers, but also great people. However, I do have a gut feeling that George Cole has never sung again.

My two-week job turned into more than a year's job. Again, as replacements came in, I went back to England and worked with everyone coming into the show. One interesting time was when Sarah Brightman was hired to play the part of Kate. After Sarah married Andrew Lloyd Webber and became a big star, Annie Ross reminded me that I had worked with her to put her into *Pirates*. I didn't even remember her!! The British actors and actresses are so well-disciplined and aware of the responsibilities of the theater that I always found it a pleasure to work with them.

# ♪ Chapter Thirteen ♫

## My Challenge

*"I do what I can"*
*~Bette Midler*

♪

In 1982, after Carl, my companion, passed away, I soon developed a condition called "spasmodic dysphonia." My father had become more frail in California and I was flying there often and was pretty stressed out from all the work and traveling. So whether that had anything to do with this vocally debilitating problem, we probably will never know.

According to the doctors, it can be caused by a bad case of the flu, by a difficult trauma, or by anything else that throws off the neurological system. The easiest way to explain it is to say that it is a form of Parkinson's disease, but is localized in one area of the body. Naturally, as a singer and vocal teacher, wouldn't you know that it would hit in the most vulnerable place—the throat and vocal cords. It is a spasm of the vocal cords and makes the tone stop and start without warning. It is very difficult to speak sometimes—to get a sentence out without the stoppage—so it becomes very frustrating to speak and to teach.

I refused to believe the diagnosis because I simply didn't want it to be true. It was also a very new disease and I believe that doctors sometimes get into a "fad" disease—suddenly everybody has some form of it. Just like acid reflux. In the case of spasmodic dysphonia, the doctors could offer nothing. There still is no cure today, but there is help for the symptoms.

So I ignored the problem and went on with my life and teaching. However, occasionally someone would say to me, "How can you be a voice teacher and sound like you do?" That was very hurtful for me, but I had to understand where they were coming from. I know that I lost some potential students because of it, but most of my students, including the stars, had simply gotten so used to it that it didn't bother them at all.

I could no longer demonstrate the sound that I was aiming for. I had to learn to explain and verbalize what I wanted to hear and then let the student find it for themselves. In all actuality, I do believe this has helped the student to know what they are aiming for. When they feel it, I believe they know their own technique better than simply imitating the teacher. It is faster to teach by having the student imitate the correct placement and sound, but I believe the other way has more validity for the student, and actors as well. When students are on the road in a long-run show and get into difficulties vocally, they can fix their own problem most of the time. And that is through knowing their own voice and their own technique. Occasionally someone will call me from the road, and we will figure out something together to help them over a problem that has developed over a period of time. But I really want my students to know how to handle their own instrument. It is so important to feel confident in what you are doing.

# ♪ Chapter Fourteen ♫

## More Shows and Singers

*"One of the things wrong with our business
is that a lot of people are desperate to "make it."
You have to take pleasure in the process"*
*~James Lipton, Host of "Inside the Actors Studio"*

# Marge Rivingston

♪

Something I believe we have lost in this country is the art of building careers. At that time in London, and it has changed some now, you began in the chorus, graduated to small parts and on to leading roles or into other avenues of acting, such as movies and television. We are too star-oriented and sometimes allow people who do not actually have the training for the theater, singing or dancing to be hired for leading roles that should be given to the performers who have prepared themselves to do those roles.

It is unfortunate today that the theater, as a whole, is all about real estate. That is what Joe Papp used to say and why he did not care to be a Broadway producer. The only thing that seems to count is filling every seat in the house for every performance. So, some very good plays and musicals go down the tubes because they are not supported and kept open by the producers. However, once in a while, a producer comes along who truly loves theater and also has a good business sense and can bring these two things together. When that happens, great theater gets produced.

Another thing that used to exist was a lot of summer stock where one could get hired to do a series of shows and get lots of experience working onstage with a live audience. That way one could learn acting skills while performing. A kind of "on-the-job training." There is not much left of stock companies these days, but we do have good regional theaters where one can get good experience. I know that acting teachers around the country will not appreciate my viewpoint, but I believe that most of acting is learned through doing. So getting a job and doing your on-the-job training is a really quick way to learn your craft.

A few more shows were in the schedule. One that I truly adored and never got tired of was *Me and My Girl*. What a fun show—and such great British humor. I worked with people in the Broadway company and on the road. Again, with Tim Curry who was wonderful in the crazy part of Bill Snibson.

As my name grew as a teacher in NYC, more people showed up who wanted to work with me. James Taylor came for a while. He is such a decent man and so willing to learn more about his craft.

68

♪

I had the great pleasure of working with Meryl Streep for almost a year on *Evita*, as we thought she was going to be the one to make the movie. That, of course, did not happen, but I do remember Meryl saying to me that she thought Madonna was the perfect choice for that part. Sure enough it turned out that way. Being a real Broadway devotee, I always thought that it was most unfair to Patti LuPone that they didn't hire her for the movie, since she had originated the part on Broadway.

Meryl was a total joy to work with because of her ability to focus. When Meryl entered my studio for an hour lesson, there was nothing else going on with her except her total attention to me and what she was doing with her voice. No business calls, no husband or children talk—just total concentration for that hour on what she was learning and applying. No wonder she and Joe Papp had such a wonderful relationship. They both had the ability to concentrate totally on the moment.

What a lesson for all of us, especially for me. I've frankly never been that good at staying in the moment. I have to really work at it, as I think most people do. My mind tends to wander into other areas rather than stay with the thoughts and problems of the present.

Another one of my favorite people that I worked with during that time was the actor Ron Liebman. I'm sure he would not say he was a singer, but we did a takeoff on the opera *Don Pasquale* in Central Park one summer and he was great. But the interesting thing about Ron is that for years, and I mean years, he has always used his old vocalizing tape to warm up for big acting parts. I saw him in *Rumors* on Broadway and he said he always warmed up with the singing tape, as he had so much hard speaking to do in that play. However, when I suggested that we get together and make a new tape, he did not seem very enthusiastic. I decided that his old tape must have felt like a comfortable old shoe, and he did not want to mess with a sure thing. So I imagine he is still doing his old tape. I hope he made copies of it, because it certainly would be worn out by now. It's a good idea to make extra copies of your favorite tape.

The 1983 musical revival of *Zorba* was done with Anthony Quinn and Lila Kadrova, and I was asked by the producers Fran and Barry

Weisler to work with Anthony on his singing. A great actor but not much of a singer. The composer John Kander and the lyricist Fred Ebb wrote a beautiful new song for the production. We went to work on the new song and the entire score. Now, Anthony was a very egotistical person and expected the world to revolve around his wishes. This was okay except that I was so busy then that I had to arrange time for him to come to my place, and what he really wanted was for me to drop everything and come to his place. We seemed to work that out fairly well, and I did go to his place part of the time. I think he rather enjoyed the lessons and learning how to speak-sing (sprechtstimme).

Then Lila wanted to work on her songs and she was such a delight—a consummate actress and performer. We got along so well and continued to stay in touch for years after *Zorba*. But, one day in rehearsal, I came to work with both Lila and Anthony at the theater and made the unforgivable error of continuing to work with Lila when he was ready to work. Lila and I only needed a few minutes to finish the work we were doing on one of the songs, but that was a no-no. He was the "star." He flew into a rage and had me fired from the production.

The producers had promised that I would be coming on the road to tend to everyone's vocal needs as they moved the show from city to city—the sort of thing I had done on *Pirates*. The producers had a great way to get out of that agreement and not have to pay me to go on the road. It was not a pleasant outcome for me. One of my students was in the chorus and so they used her to warm up Anthony on the road. It was an extra bonus for her, as she got paid to do that job. So goes show business!

Somewhere in the midst of all this hoopla, *Little Shop of Horrors* was being done in London. Once again, Ellen Greene insisted that I be with her for the rehearsals, so off I went to London again. I was so happy to spend a little more time there, and my boss this time was Cameron Mackintosh. He wasn't so successful a producer at that time and had a very small office in London where I went to get my paycheck. He was not very happy about the arrangement with Ellen Greene. He didn't like having to pay me, so it was a bit uncomfortable to go there and wait for him to sign my paycheck. Today I'm sure that would not be a problem because he is one of the biggest musical producers in the world.

I also met an exceptional voice teacher in London at that time. Her name was Florence Norberg. I wanted Ellen to have someone to work with when I left, and she did see her once or twice. I found Florence Norberg to be such an interesting person besides being an exceptional voice teacher. But one day when I visited her (and we sat and shared a glass of sherry together), one thing she said to me made such an impression on me that I have included it in every article and statement I have ever written about the voice. It was this: "The voice is the only instrument that cannot be replaced. We should have more respect for it!" Amen!

Christine Ebersole showed up here somewhere in time as they were doing a workshop production of a musical version of *It's a Wonderful Life*. The musical director brought her to my studio, and we worked on the songs. What a delightful and talented person. We had a great time working on the material, but the show did not get past the workshop stage. I thought it should go on, but the backing wasn't there. Not enough money to mount a production. This happens so often. Material that is really good and interesting never gets put on in a theater. (Christine has such a great natural instrument that I used to have to think up things to make her work or she would not have vocalized at all. I never told her this. If she ever reads this book, she will be surprised. Happily, I hope.)

# ♪ Chapter Fifteen ♫

## More Teaching

*"I am enough of an artist to draw freely upon my imagination.*
*Imagination is more important than knowledge.*
*Knowledge is limited.*
*Imagination encircles the world"*
*~Albert Einstein*

♪

One of my greatest theater events was working with Natalia Makarova—the great ballerina. She did a revival of *On Your Toes*, with George Abbott directing just as he had done many years previous. He was in his nineties then and it was such a pleasure and privilege to watch him work with the leading actors and the whole cast. He never put anyone down, and he had such patience and love for the theater that it was inspiring to be near him.

Natalia did not speak very good English and she had to learn how to speak her lines. She was a very disciplined person, as you can imagine, being the great ballerina that she was. We did our lessons religiously and she did a very nice job in the show. Of course, the outstanding moment was her dancing of *Slaughter on Tenth Avenue*. The music was written by Richard Rodgers and it was one of his best theatrical numbers. She was brilliant dancing this part, but at the first performance (I believe it was in Washington, D.C.) in the middle of the dance, a piece of scenery fell—or something fell from the rafters—and almost hit her. What a scary thing that was. She could easily have been killed or badly injured. The chances one takes in the theater.

The reason I got to work with her and be involved with the show was through George Irving—a brilliant Broadway performer and a great singer. We used to work on some German Lieder (art songs) together, along with Broadway material. When he heard that Natalia needed a coach, he suggested me and that was terrific for me. One funny and poignant memory I have is that during rehearsals in the theater, Mr. Abbott would be sitting in the theater, would try to get up out of his seat to go up to the stage and correct something or change something, and would not be able to get his legs to hold him up very well for a few seconds. Remember, he was in his nineties. So we would all hold our breath and pray he wouldn't fall in the aisle. He never wanted help, so we would just wait till his legs started to work and then he would walk on up to the stage and give his direction. It was so sweet to watch him trying to be strong and physically capable of directing a show. I will never forget him or the experience itself. He was still quite capable for that job.

Somewhere during this time of my teaching life, I got a telephone call from someone wanting to take voice lessons from me. Now, to understand my "type A" personality, you have to picture that the particular day that I received this call was on a Friday late afternoon when I was tired and wanting to finish up teaching for the day. This rather timid voice said that she was interested in taking lessons from me. When she said she was calling from Nashville, I was a little short with her on the phone. I said, "How do you expect to do this?"—or something to that effect. I said to call me back on Saturday morning and I would talk with her then. When she pronounced her name, I understood it as "Roxanne Katz." I certainly did not know of anyone by that name. So, later on that evening, I was talking to one of my students on the phone and I told her about the call. She really blew up at me and said, "That was Rosanne Cash, you dummy." Oops! Did I feel foolish. So you can imagine that my attitude was somewhat different when she called me on Saturday morning.

She did come to New York with her husband at that time, Rodney Crowell, and they both worked with me for years when in New York. Rosanne is so talented and such a nice person, and for many years we have kept in touch. I don't know that she knows that story at all, so she may get a big kick out of it when she reads this book. I certainly hope the humor is not lost on her!

Also during this period of high-profile teaching, another wonderful person came into my life as a student and friend—Jane Powell. What a lovely lady and talented person. We worked very hard to get her voice in shape to do some shows that she wanted to do. She was getting a lot of work at that time doing symphony dates and her own one-woman show. Remembering her beautiful sound in the movies was a great help to me in directing her vocal exercises to accomplish more of what her real sound had been. She had been doing some belting-type roles, such as Nellie Forbush in *South Pacific* and some others. Her voice did not sit in that register naturally, so she had lost some of her high voice.

It is very hard in this business when you are contracted to do roles that are not so natural to your own sound. Most of the time, the performer does not really understand that and assumes that if you are a singer you can do any type of singing. Not so. At least not without some help and direction. Remember that!

We started to work very lightly in trying to find the upper register again, and one day Jane said to me, "How can we get the voice to respond to the high notes again?" I just said, "We trick it." That was my way of saying that we do different things vocally to get the voice to respond to the sound she used to have. I also asked her to look at her movies and listen to her singing in order to reacquaint herself with that sound that was still inside her. It was there; it just needed to be brought out again.

This all worked quite well for her, and we both felt good and encouraged by her vocal improvement and ability to sing the things that she wanted to and was well-known for. You realize that once you have an established reputation—some hit songs or movies—you always have to do those numbers when performing with an orchestra or on a program of your own. Your audience never gets tired of hearing those songs that they love to hear you sing. You may be sick to death of them, but that does not matter. The audience is what matters. So you do them over and over again.

Jane and I became friends, and I even spent a wonderful Christmas Day with her and her husband, Dick Moore, at their adorable home in Connecticut. Speaking of Dick Moore, about that time he asked me to write an article on "the voice" for the fiftieth anniversary of *AFTRA* magazine. In case you don't know what that stands for, it is "American Federation of Television and Radio Actors." I said that I wasn't sure I could write anything for actors, but I would try.

I went up to my cabin in the Pocono Mountains where there would be no distractions, and I sat down at my trusty old typewriter (in those days) and started to write about how to use and keep the voice healthy throughout a long and varied career.

But first, here's a quick story about how the cabin got built. In 1979, I wanted to invest some money in property and I wanted the property to be by the ocean. My friend and musical director Kevin Farrell owned a place in Jamestown, Rhode Island. There was a large house and a small cottage on the property. The cottage was right on the water and overlooked the Newport Bridge, which is something to see—absolutely beautiful. But it was a little far from New York City, and the cottage needed a lot of work. Carl, my companion at that time, saw it and didn't think I should buy it. A few months later, Kevin called and asked, "How would a lake do?" So Carl and I went to see that property in Pennsylvania, just beyond the Delaware Water Gap Bridge—two hours from New York City. The property was beautiful, with a little private lake (not on any map) called Crescent Lake. Within a year, I was dying to build on the property, and we did—my beautiful cabin where I spent many weekends over the next ten years.

Back to my article for *AFTRA* magazine, I thought it ended up being useful for actors as well as singers. The title of the article was "Can the Voice Do It All?" (It can be found in Appendix II.) It did indeed appear in the magazine and I was very proud of the reactions that I received from actors.

I also worked with Carrie Fisher when she was doing *Agnes of God* on Broadway. She is a very talented person in so many areas and singing was one of them. However, she used to say to me that her mother (Debbie Reynolds) was the singer, so Carrie always stayed in the background with her singing. I felt it was too bad that she did not develop that talent as well as her acting and writing talents. But a funny and smart lady she is.

Another show came along around that time called *Harrigan and Hart*. It starred Mark Hamill and Harry Groener. Mark Hamill you will remember as Luke Skywalker in *Star Wars*. The show was directed by Joe Layton who was a pretty big-name director on Broadway at that time. I didn't get to know him very well, but later on I found that he had directed Bette Midler's shows, and I did get to know him on *Experience the Divine Bette Midler* that Bette toured with after we finished the TV movie of *Gypsy*.

Joe Layton was a very talented director and knew how to work with actors. Unfortunately, *Harrigan and Hart* did not fill every seat in the theater every performance, so it closed within a couple of weeks. What a shame. Mark was delightful to work with and very versatile with his talent.

I worked with Harry Groener later on when he replaced Mandy Patinkin in *Sunday in the Park with George*. That was a killer score to sing. Mandy had originated the show and had such a unique range and ability that it was hard for anyone to replace him. Harry was wonderful though. A very good actor and a very good singer. He went on to originate a wonderful singing and dancing Gershwin show called *Crazy for You*, where he had to really dance, sing and act. What we call a "triple threat" in the business.

Kate Burton (Richard Burton's daughter) was also doing a musical around that time and I had the pleasure of working with her and getting to know her. She inherited a lot of her father's acting ability and is a delightful person to know and to work with. A very serious actress. The name of the show was *Doonsbury* and it was based on the cartoon by Gary Trudeau. It was delightful, with a brilliant cast of characters and actors, but once again, it did not run terribly long. Kate and I continued to work together on her singing for some time to come, but she went on to do many more wonderful acting roles and I don't think she ever did another singing role.

# ♪ Chapter Sixteen ♫

## Vocal Class Work

*"The creation of something new*
*is not accomplished by the intellect,*
*But the play instinct,*
*Acting from inner necessity"*
*~Carl G. Jung*

# Marge Rivingston

♪

During this period of the '80s, I decided that something was missing with my students, because they were not getting the jobs that I thought they were totally qualified for. So, with my friend David Friedman, who was a Broadway conductor at that time, I decided that we should have a three-hour open class where my students and any other singers who were interested could come and get up on their feet and sing their audition material for us. Then we could see what was not coming through in their auditions. This made sense to us because we knew that what a student did in a private lesson was not necessarily what they would or could do under audition circumstances.

Sure enough, we found a lot of answers. People tightened up so much that they looked almost frozen standing there trying to get through their song. For me, and probably why I came up with this process, I remembered only too well that I would audition for a role, and when I would finish the audition, I would say good-bye to the people behind the table, walk out, and feel as though I had no idea what I had just sung or how it had sounded. Had I cracked on a high note? Oh, I guess I would have remembered that. But, generally speaking, I did not know how poorly or how well I had actually sung—or how I had presented myself, for that matter. All of that counts in an audition—how you come across to the "powers that be" who sit behind that table.

The only way I knew how the audition had gone was if I got the job. However, here's another common frustrating experience in the business: Sometimes you feel that you have done well, one of the people from behind that table comes over to you and tells you *what a wonderful job* you did and practically offers you the job on the spot, says they will call you, and then you never hear from them. That is one of the really hurtful rejections you have to face. It is almost better when they say thank you and you don't expect to hear from them, and then the next day you get a call from your agent saying that they want you to do the part. Wow, that is terrific.

So, back to David's and my class. We worked with each individual about ten or fifteen minutes on one song. It was such a revelation to us how nerves affected the auditioner's singing and personality when they got up to sing. Relaxation, awareness of the body, and breath control became our goal in getting people to appear to be "present" at their own audition. (You all know about being "present" or being "in the moment," don't you? It is sad if you cannot enjoy the moment, even though it is fraught with terror and uncertainty.)

David and I collaborated beautifully in this effort and it was well worth our time to help singers realize their own potential. Emotions sometimes took over and people broke down and cried because they felt so inadequate and insecure. I think one has to realize that performing comes from the core of one's emotions that sit right in the middle of the body and are directly affected by the breath. So, if you are feeling insecure or inadequate in the material you are attempting to do and you relate to that feeling honestly, you will probably start crying. It is really an important breakthrough when that happens. Students will say, "Well, I can't get up there and fall apart in the middle of an audition," and that is right. However, if you allow yourself to feel your true feelings within a particular song, you may go through three, four or five times of falling apart before you can honestly feel the emotion but not fall apart from it. It is a process, and a painful one at times, but it allows you, as the interpreter, to let the audience feel the true emotions of the song. It takes a lot of trust to let yourself go, and that is the sign of a great performer. This class turned out to be exactly what I wanted it to be—a step in between the security of a private lesson and the pressure of walking into an audition for a job. It worked and helped many people get jobs.

Later on I did refine the class and included body work, relaxation techniques, centering exercises, and vocalizations. That class was even more successful for people than the open class. It was limited to eight people for a three-hour class. That meant that I had ample time with each person to explore the entire sphere of a song. I had a Trager body worker, Roger Tolle, with me and he took the first part of the class to teach students how to prepare to sing, to audition, and to do a show eight times a week.

Roger was wonderful, generous and kind to everyone and we had great success with teaching this method of preparation and centering oneself before attempting to sing. I also had Skip Kennon as my accompanist and coach to help people get the most out of the music and interpretation of a piece. Now you may ask what I was doing in this class. I would say that I was just there helping to put it all together and direct the students into the best sounds vocally that they could make in a piece of material. But it was such a collaborative effort that each one of us had our individual parts to play and it all worked so well together for the benefit of the student. We did some version of these classes for about seven years before I moved to California.

# ♪ Chapter Seventeen ♫

## Shows Continue

*"To strive, to seek, to find, and not yield"*
*~Alfred Lord Tennyson*

♪

Now where was I? Another show came along by Andrew Lloyd Webber. That was *Joseph and His Amazing Technicolor Dreamcoat*. In my opinion it is the most delightful show he has ever written. As I understand it, he wrote it early in his career and it was conceived as a children's show. The characters are so well written, and keeping the Bible story totally intact is not an easy thing to do. But the lead part of Joseph was a rather hard tenor part to sing. And once again, my friend David Friedman was the conductor. He realized that Bill Hutton was having some trouble with all of the high notes in the role and suggested that I work with Bill on the part. That was the beginning of a long relationship with *Joseph*.

I truly love the show and never get tired of seeing or hearing it. It can be done very professionally or it can be done in little theaters with a local cast and it still holds together beautifully. During the Broadway run of the show, the lead part changed quite a few times and I worked with most of those replacements. The interesting part was that all of the Cassidy brothers played the part at one time or another. David was the first replacement and he was great in the show. Next was Patrick whom I had worked with as Frederic in *Pirates*. Next came Shaun, and I worked with him a little. They are all delightful talents and very dedicated to their art.

Now, you may be getting the idea that I was a little busy during this time of my career as a teacher. I was also learning how to work with stars and with both women and men performers. Some teachers think that it is very different to teach a woman and then a man, but as I will discuss later, I found so many similarities vocally that it was quite easy for me to be able to teach both sexes. During that time I actually bought the book *Burned Out* because I felt like I was becoming pretty burned out with all the demands on me. I guess that did not stop me from continuing on my chosen path, but I think I learned how to take some time for myself when I needed to.

More shows in the '80s included *Big River*, which was a beautiful and wonderful show. The score by Roger Miller fit the story of *Huck Finn* so beautifully that it seemed an almost seamless production between the dialogue and the music. Daniel Jenkins was the first Huck and he was so young and right for the part. He needed a little help vocally, and I was asked to do that and to help him develop the stamina to sing the role eight times a week. Some of our old gang was there, including Patricia McGourty doing costumes as she had on *Pirates*, Linda Twine the conductor, and Des McAnuff the director.

I had known Des when he was a very young, very enthusiastic writer and director at the Public Theater. Another one of those young talents that Joe Papp helped support. A talented cast included Patti Cohenour, again from *Pirates*, and Jennifer Leigh Warren from *Little Shop of Horrors*. So I had a ball with everyone. The company seemed to all get along like family and that is a real pleasure in the theater. It does not always happen that way, believe me. *Big River* opened on Broadway in 1985 and was a huge success. It enjoyed a long run and won the Tony for best musical that year.

# ♪ Chapter Eighteen ♫

## La Boheme

*"Only those who risk going too far*
*can possibly find out how far one can go"*
*~T.S. Eliot*

♪

Just now I am remembering another experience, a totally different type of experience in the theater. I believe this was in 1983. You remember that I mentioned before how much Linda Ronstadt admired Joe Papp. Well, the test of that admiration was on. Joe suggested he would like to do a small, intimate version of the opera *La Boheme* in English at the Public Theater. Wow! Linda said yes and so we went to work again. Now what you need to know here is that Linda is a fabulous singer and has an extraordinary ear, but she does not read music. Here we are talking about a large, leading operatic role that she had to learn note by note and phrase by phrase. Also, learning her musical entrances was one of the really difficult things about the score. So I am plunking out notes and phrases on the piano and working on the vocal part while she is also listening to recordings of the opera.

During this period of time, Linda was dating George Lucas, and he and Steven Spielberg wanted to go on vacation to Hawaii. They had just finished a movie. I can't tell you which one, but they wanted to get away for a couple of weeks. Linda told George that she could not go with them because of her commitment to learn the score with me for *La Boheme*. George said, "That isn't a problem. Just bring Marge along and we will find a piano and you will work on the music every day." So I was invited to go to Hawaii with this famous gang. We flew from Burbank to Hawaii on a private jet belonging to one of the studios—some way to travel. I could have gotten spoiled, but I had to eventually come back to earth and what I could afford after that.

We stayed on the Big Island of Hawaii at the Mauna Kea resort. My suite was so large that I couldn't possibly have used all that space during the time that I was there, but it was terrific. The other part of this story is that Steven Spielberg and Amy Irving had just gotten back together after having broken up a few years before. So Amy was with us too. What a group. Amy loved sports, which did not seem to be Steven's thing at all, so she went wind surfing, rode horseback, and I did not see much of her at all except at mealtime.

What George and Steven did was build sandcastles all day, and they were beautiful—large with unique designs. Everyone pretty much left them alone at the resort and they were happy with the arrangement. Linda and I did our work every day and accomplished so much while I was there. Every once in a while she would say she did not feel like working that day. Not with George Lucas around, I can tell you that. He would just say to Linda, "Go do your work," and that was that. They were all so generous to me and always called me before dinnertime to include me in whatever plans they had made for the evening.

One night I did decide to go on a sunset cruise, which none of them wanted to do. So they let me take the car and I went off by myself. I was very used to traveling alone at that time and I really wanted to see something more of the area than they were interested in. I imagine they had all been there before and it was a relaxation time for them, but I wanted to do some sightseeing. On the cruise, everyone knew who I was and who I was with, so I got all of the questions that they wanted to ask but had been very nice not to bother the group with. It was a magical kind of time for me, and I loved my time in Hawaii.

I had a friend living on Maui, and George bought me a first-class ticket to get there and back to L.A. That was something new for me. I decided I liked that way of traveling. I got to spend two days on Maui, and I loved the beauty there.

A few weeks later, rehearsals began in New York City. Linda was overwhelmed by the magnitude of what she had agreed to do. Acting was not her forte, and she felt somewhat insecure in that area. Gary Morris was the Rudolfo, and he was a country singer. But what a gorgeous voice he possessed. He could sing the *La Boheme* score beautifully. A real natural gift. Neither one of them was an actor, but they were so honest, sweet and endearing as Mimi and Rudolfo that everyone loved the production.

Early on, during rehearsals, it was decided that Linda could not do eight shows a week of *La Boheme*. (It would be miraculous if *any* soprano could sing a Puccini opera eight times a week.) Opera singers sing a maximum of only three performances a week, and even though this was a small production, the music was still done with the complete score. So,

♪

once again, we hired Patti Cohenour to do three shows a week. We also hired Caroline Peyton to stand by and do occasional performances, so we had our old group together again. What fun those years were for me— working with such talented and dedicated people. Bill Elliot and Wilfred Leach, the musical director and stage director from *Pirates*, were at the helm again.

Gary Morris never actually worked with me during *La Boheme*, but he saw me at the theater every day and night, so we got to know each other pretty well. Almost every performance I would hear him having trouble on one high G, but I didn't think it was my place to say anything to him or try to give him advice about how he could get that note. But I could see that it made him uncomfortable, so one night I got up the courage to go to his dressing room after the performance and say to him, "If you would change the position of your tongue on that vowel and relax it forward against the bottom teeth, I think you would find the sound that you want and not be hung up on that note every night." He said, "Thanks. It has really been bothering me. I'll try it your way." Well, he did and was so happy when the problem disappeared. Later on I saw him do *Les Miz* in New York, and I thought he was absolutely wonderful in that part.

One interesting recollection during *La Boheme* was the night that Placido Domingo came to see the show. He was a big fan of Linda's and later on they did some singing together for benefits. Well, Linda thought she was terrible in the show, but afterward in her dressing room, Placido came in and told her how wonderful it was to see a small, intimate production of *La Boheme*. He gave Linda such compliments on her singing and how she acted the part so honestly that we all felt really good. He also complimented me on my work with Linda, and that was a very nice feeling for me. I have always been a huge fan of his, so it meant a lot to me that he thought I had been able to guide Linda in her singing of a very tough operatic role. I have to say that Linda was relieved when the run of that show was over. But I still believe the production was a big success.

# ♪ Chapter Nineteen ♫

## Linda, Emmy Lou and Dolly

*"Imagination is everything.*
*It is the preview of life's coming attractions"*
*~Albert Einstein*

When Linda went home to Los Angeles, she started to work with Nelson Riddle on a recording of standards. That was the greatest collaboration. Nelson Riddle was well-known for his arrangements for all the big pop singers of that day—and for good reason. His chord structures and rhythms were unique and interesting to listen to. Linda adored him, and he adored her. He was like a father to her and also a mentor. She didn't have a lot of style for that music and he really taught her how to use her voice in the style of the old forties music. Of course I grew up with that music, so when Linda told me that she had heard this beautiful song called "Skylark," I just cracked up. That music opened up her voice so much and developed her love for another style of music—trying new things vocally and stylistically. She is still experimenting with new instruments and arrangements.

Three albums came out of that collaboration, and they were all outstanding. The first one was *What's New* in 1983. Then came *Lush Life* in 1984. When it came time to record the last one, *For Sentimental Reasons*, in 1985, Nelson Riddle was very ill and passed away before the album was finished. It was hard for Linda to go back into the studio and finish that recording without him there. She finally did, and it turned out very well. I had said to her that she had learned all the style of that music from Nelson, and she owed it to him to get in the studio and finish the album. Today her voice is still fresh and beautiful, richer and more full-bodied than it has ever been.

We continue to work whenever we can get together, and one thing that we do is phone lessons. Now that always strikes everyone as pretty strange, but it allows me to hear what she is doing and to guide her into a good warm-up when she is going out to sing. I only do this when I have worked with someone a lot and I know what kind of problems they get into and how I can still give some direction to their warm-up, even over the telephone. Bette Midler and I have done it for years too. I have given phone lessons on a train, in a limo, and in a taxi. And as far away as Australia.

Linda, Dolly Parton, and Emmylou Harris had always talked

♪

*Emmylou Harris & Marge*

about trying to get a time that they were all free enough of other commitments to make a record together. It finally happened and was a big success. The record is called *Trio*. A few years ago they all decided to try to do another one. Things were going along pretty well, but Linda called me and asked me to come up from Los Angeles to San Francisco and work with her and Emmylou. Now, Dolly did not want any part of this voice lesson business. So when I arrived at the recording studio, I started working with Emmylou. Some of the harmonies were not working quite the way they wanted them to—they were very close harmonies and intricate to manage. You really had to be in perfect tune to be able to blend with the other singers.

We worked and were having a good time discussing vocal techniques when Dolly arrived. She came in wearing her usual outfit of black leather jacket and pants and the highest stiletto heels I have ever seen. She was a lot of fun and told stories about her life growing up and her family. The funny thing was that everyone else was dressed so casually because here you are working in a sound studio, and it is often quite cold. But Dolly just stood up there and did her singing. She didn't seem to be as involved with the project as Linda and Emmylou were, but she was contributing her part.

Emmylou is a lady of the first order and a great performer. She is such a nice person and is willing to learn from anyone she respects. That has kept us in contact over the years, and we get together and do vocal work when her schedule allows it.

However, not long after I was up there working with them, Dolly pulled out of the project. It was a big letdown for Emmylou and Linda as they had spent so much time and energy and money getting this record together, so there were some pretty hard feelings going on. But Dolly was very busy, was very much in demand at that time, and felt that she did not have the time to give to this project. My own personal feeling about the whole thing is that Dolly didn't really believe that the record could or would make a lot of money.

Later on, in 1999, they got back together, straightened out all their personal feelings, and got busy and finished the album. It was called *Trio II*. It turned out to be quite good, and it did make a lot of money. One would assume that those three voices would not blend at all, but they blended so beautifully that it is a surprise to everyone when they hear the album. The girls always knew they would sing well together. It is a very unusual recording.

# ♪ Chapter Twenty ♫

## Decision Time

*"You create your own universe as you go along"*
*~Sir Winston Churchill*

# Marge Rivingston

♪

Backtracking a bit to 1990, I made the decision that it was time for New York and me to separate ourselves. I loved New York and my work so much that it was a hard decision to make, but it had taken a toll on me physically and emotionally. During the years that Roger Tolle and I were teaching class, he also became my massage therapist. He certainly realized the toll that all this work was taking on my body.

During my heyday years in New York, many people had always asked me to write a book about my experiences with the theater and the people with whom I had worked, but there was no energy or time to devote to that project. It had also been brought up to me to start a school that would have singing teachers who had been trained by me to teach my method. Now, I don't even know that I call it a "method," since I work differently with different students and their individual problems. And the last thing in the world that I wanted to be was an administrator of a school for singing, so I quickly passed on that idea.

In a way it is probably too bad that I didn't train more people to teach than I did, but on the other hand, the people that I did try to influence toward my beliefs about teaching have gone out on their own and developed their own techniques. And that is no surprise. Every teacher eventually should develop his or her own method and way of handling the students who come for singing lessons.

It is a very hard thing to convey the messages of how you do what you do at the time you do it and with the person you are working with. Sound complicated? It is. But, I believe one of the reasons for my success with all kinds of singers was that I tried to work with everything they had that was good, and gently introduce other ideas to improve what was not so good. I have been told many times that I possess a wonderful way of explaining what one should do without it sounding like I am a tyrant and wanting things my way only. (That has always been the furthest thing from my mind.) I always say to a student that the technique is for them and their career and that is the reason they must understand why they are doing what I am asking them to do.

Of course, we know that there are basic rules in singing, just as there are in dance and acting and art of any kind. Oddly, with the art of singing, everyone assumes, for some unknown reason, that singers should be perfect every time they open their mouth and make a sound. It just isn't so, and it puts a tremendous burden on the singer. The student usually develops throat tension trying to produce the "perfect tone."

Dancers do their barre and would not think of going onstage without a proper warm-up. I relate a lot of singing ideas to dance because of the discipline of dance and the knowledge that dancers have of their bodies. Yes, there is a God-given voice for a few, but there are many performers who have just worked hard to develop their own abilities. Those are the ones I love to teach because they have such a strong desire to improve and build their voices. Often, they are the ones who end up with the job instead of the so-called "more talented" people.

The singer opens his or her mouth and has a perfect sound come out. What a concept—nothing realistic about it. And here is the point of contention I have with some voice teachers. They expect the student to make only beautiful sounds. That is so scary to most students. How can a student live up to that expectation when they have come to the teacher for vocal help? Why would you take singing lessons if you could always make beautiful sounds? Of course you wouldn't. But that is a burden that is put on many students, and there is no way they can do their work and improve under those circumstances.

I believe in making light of mistakes while learning any craft, so that you don't beat yourself up for not being perfect. Perfect never happens anyway. I do not believe that we are put on this earth to reach perfection, but only to strive for the best each one of us can accomplish. That is all God asks of any of us.

# ♪ Chapter Twenty-One ♫

## Teaching Philosophy

"A true teacher does not impose their will on others
but makes their understandings available to all.
The teacher's function is to inspire, to instruct
and to confirm by personal testimony the truth of the teaching
and to encourage students who are struggling with the path.
The teacher provides explanation & clarification"
~David Hawkins, MD, PhD

♪

Sometimes, teachers also tend to have a personal problem with teaching instead of performing. Many teachers are or have been performers, but when they have been disappointed in their own performing careers, they tend to take it out on a student. I had a teacher like that once. There was no way that she truly wanted me to succeed where she had not succeeded. Lots of mixed messages in that teacher/ student relationship.

When you get a student whom you recognize as being much more talented than you are, believe me, it is not easy to get that large thing we call "ego" out of the way. I had my own battle with it when I made the decision to stop running around performing and instead put all my time and energies into teaching. I loved performing, but I also am a person who loves stability. That is hard to find in the performing world. My decision was a conscious knowing that I was not being fair to my students to always be leaving for weeks at a time. So for about the first three years I would go to the theater and sit there and criticize people's performances. Saying, of course, that if I had the opportunity to do that part, I would do a much better job than that person was doing.

However, once my students were out there on the Broadway stage and around the country performing, I found such joy and deep satisfaction in their being allowed to realize their potential that I gave up that "ego" part. Besides, I have always felt that I received much more applause and adulation as a teacher than I ever did as a performer.

But being a performer certainly adds value in teaching. You know the territory and you know the terror, so you can be much more empathetic and giving to the student who is experiencing these emotions and feelings of inadequacy or unworthiness.

Performers and artists of all kinds are so hard on themselves. They are so willing to believe the bad about themselves and their talent that they tend to put aside all the good. This reveals itself particularly when reading your own reviews. I know artists who won't read their own reviews. (But, you know, they always find out what is in the review anyway. Some kind soul will always tell them, particularly if it tears the artist down.)

And when we *do* read our reviews, we skip over all the good stuff and concentrate only on that "one bad line" the reviewer put in about our performance. I know this is so.

When Bette Midler was doing Radio City Music Hall in 1993 and the reviews came out, she said she was not going to read them. (However, as I told you before, someone always lets you in on what the reviews say, or they post them on the bulletin board at the theater, and it is pretty hard not to find out what is in them.) When I came backstage at Radio City the next day after the reviews had come out, she said to me, "Well, you should feel good; you got all the reviews." Now that meant that the reviews were all about how well she was singing, and she was very happy about that. Even if I did get all the reviews. It was her way of thanking me for the help that I had given her vocally. Of course that is an exaggeration, but it was fun and Bette did it in a happy way. I was with her for the first week at Radio City and warming her up every night for the show.

The most outstanding thing about that show was that she did a six-week run at Radio City Music Hall, which seats over five thousand people a performance, and she sold out the entire six weeks. What a tribute to her as an artist and entertainer. She is wonderful in movies and in what television she has done, but her true forte is performing live for a live audience. She has an energy that is unbelievable on the stage. You realize that in person she is not very tall, but on that stage she seems to be larger than life. The audiences love her.

# ♪ Chapter Twenty-Two ♫

## Move to California

*"Never confuse your self worth
with your professional success or failure"*
*~Cherry Jones, Actor, Tony Winner*

## Marge Rivingston

♪

After I moved to California in 1991, a friend told me that there was now someone who could help the symptoms for the spasmodic dysphonia. That someone was Dr. Daniel Truong at the University of California, Irvine Medical Center. I had an interview with him, and he confirmed the diagnosis of spasmodic dysphonia. He said that he could help the symptoms to disappear with a shot of Botox®. I had to go to a voice lab where they measured the spasms and where they occurred in the vocal cords, and then Dr. Truong was able to know exactly where to put the shot to stop the spasms.

Now that Botox is popular for cosmetic procedures, it is well known to most people. At that time it was fairly new, and I had never heard the word before. The shot itself is very scary because it is a long needle going into the throat from the outside. Sort of straight through the larynx. They shoot a very small dose of Botox into the cords and it releases the spasms for a certain period of time.

What an amazing thing this has been for me. Especially for teaching, and for life in general. My symptoms would be gone for up to six months at a time, so I only had to have the shot twice a year. I was actually able to sing some after the shots and demonstrate again, so it has been a real blessing in my life. I have much more sensitivity toward any throat problems that a student might have, and I feel that I also have the knowledge to help other people when something like this appears in their lives.

Now, when I am giving a voice lesson, it seems to go something like this: I teach forty-five minutes of psychology and fifteen minutes of voice production. Let me explain: We all know that when something is hurting you or you are emotionally upset, the last thing in the world you can do or feel like doing is sing. I believe that is because the emotions are seated in the breath and the diaphragm. Just think back for a moment to a time when you were very hurt or emotionally upset, and observe what you do. Usually you hold your breath. The breath releases so much feeling and emotion that you will undoubtedly begin to cry if you try breathing deeply. It unleashes all the pent-up feelings that you have been trying to

104

push down and keep under control.

So, when a student would come in the door for their lesson, I could almost always tell whether they were okay or in a very vulnerable place. I would ask them, "How are you?" and they would answer, "Fine, just fine." At that point I would know that it really was not the truth. With a little prodding they would tell me what was wrong—a bad audition, losing a job, or something in their personal life. Whatever it was, they were hurting. That would start the release of tears and letting go. Then we could get on with the singing lesson.

I have always admired singers who could get up and sing at a memorial service or funeral of one of their friends and not break down. They simply become the actor and do not deal with their emotions of the moment until they have done their singing. It can be done, but I don't believe I could ever have done it. I would have been too choked up to get a decent sound out.

# ♪ Chapter Twenty-Three ♫

## Goodbye, New York City

*"Don't fulfill my expectations - Amaze Me!"*
*~Riber Hansson, Editorial Cartoonist, Sweden*

♪

Back to that momentous decision to move back to California in 1991. It had some funny moments in it. I told my students in New York that on June 1, 1991, I would be leaving New York and moving out to sunny California. I started this process almost a year before I was going to leave, and tried to have my students start thinking about another teacher. Quite a few of them never heard a word I said. They were in total denial of the fact that I would leave them. A few of them got quite angry that I was leaving, and others became very hurt. It seemed like a personal rejection to them. But when they finally realized that it was for my own good that I move, they began to calm down and deal with the truth.

*Maureen, Penny, Marge & Estelle*

And so, on June 1, 1991, I indeed did fly away to Southern California. However, before I left, I experienced one of the greatest nights of my life and work in New York City. A surprise farewell party was arranged by what had become known as "The Four Divas." That included Maureen McGovern, Estelle Parsons, Meg Bussert and Penny Worth. They put together the most fabulous evening with entertainment, amazing food and so many students and friends. I don't know how they found all the phone numbers, but we had about eighty-five people in and out of an unusually large apartment on the Upper West Side. This apartment belonged to Dan Burlinghoff, who had been the conductor of *Pirates of Penzance*. The people who could not attend sent wonderful cards and letters expressing their appreciation for me and the things I had taught them about singing. This included Kevin Kline, Treat Williams, Karla DeVito, Robby Benson, and many others. A beautiful, large and heavy book with pictures and a video were all given to me that night. We had lots of laughs and lots of tears.

The whole group had learned a song from Pirates called "Hail, Poetry." They had changed the words to fit the occasion and so the verse ended up something like this: "Hail, Ri-ving-ston, thou heav'n-born maid/ Thou gild-est long the sing-er's trade/Hail, flow-ing fount of 'n-cour-age-ment!/All hail, di-vine e-mol-li-ent." What a sound to remember in my ears. All these marvelous Broadway singers joining their voices together in praise of me. Wow!

Maureen McGovern sang a song from *On the Town* (music by Leonard Bernstein and lyrics by Comden and Green) with the line that ends with "Oh well, we'll catch up another day." It was so beautiful but a little sad. The whole evening was such a wonderful tribute to me and all that I had tried to give to my students and the shows I had been privileged to be involved with. It seems I had much love given to me that night, and even now when I return to New York, I have the feeling of being part of that wonderful world of Broadway.

*Marge & Maureen*

# ♪ Chapter Twenty-Four ♫

## Bette Midler and Gypsy

*"Success isn't Final, Failure isn't Fatal"*
*~Don Shula, Hall of Fame Head Football Coach*

♪

I had made up my mind that I did not want to live in the Los Angeles area. I wanted to live close to the beach and the ocean, so I ended up buying a place in Laguna Woods. It is terrific to be so near the ocean, which to me is such a healing and calming atmosphere. After living in a small apartment in New York City for almost forty years, it felt good to have space inside and space outside. Not being much of a gardener, it is interesting that I chose to have a place where I could have lots of plants and flowers. The end of that story is that I hired someone to make it look beautiful, and I just enjoy looking at it every day.

The only problem with my choice of where to live is that it makes it a little difficult to do a lot of teaching in the Los Angeles area. With the use of my friend Laurie Franks' Hollywood apartment, I did this trek every two weeks and taught some wonderful people, but it became increasingly difficult to drive the freeways and spend the time I needed for teaching. Some people continue to drive down here to Laguna Woods for their lessons and that works very well for me.

However, the stars that I still work with do not have the time to come this far for a lesson. It ends up to be the major part of a day, and they simply do not have that kind of time available on a weekly basis. So I do travel up to Beverly Hills to keep track of how some of my people are singing. Can't let them get too far off track!

In 1993 I read in the paper that Bette Midler was going to do a TV movie version of the Broadway show *Gypsy*. Now, not only is that one of my favorite shows, but I also had worked with other people on the role of Mama Rose, and I knew the difficulties that the role presented, particularly vocally.

Because Bette is known as a belter, I think everyone thought that the role would be a natural for her, but because the role is so vocally demanding, she wanted some help with the singing. How I got that job—and job it was—was that after I saw this in the paper, I contacted Christine Ebersole because she knew Bette's musical director, Mark Shaiman. Christine called him, and Mark told Bette that I was living in Southern California now. Bette said, "I remember her," and she called me.

♪

We started to work on the part and, as usual, had very little time to prepare before the cast began rehearsals. The tessitura, the general note range, of Mama Rose's songs is quite a high belt, because it was originally written for Ethel Merman who had a unique high belting range. (She had one of the biggest sounds I have ever heard in a Broadway theater.) We discovered that Bette had a lot of high-register notes in her voice, but they had never been developed and incorporated into her actual singing technique. She worried so much about intonation, attacks and releases that it was hard to get her breathing apparatus really working to support her sound. We worked a lot on breath and trying to bring some of the overtones of the high register down into the lower voice to keep the pitch up and also to give a fresh ring to her voice.

I can't say enough about the idea of exercising the entire instrument. The way I try to explain this is to ask the student if they would exercise just half of their body. What would happen to the other half? It doesn't matter what register you are performing in, but how you take care of the entire instrument. So if you are performing a belting role eight times a week, you had better learn to warm up the head or top voice a great deal to keep the balance in the instrument.

So Bette and I would do our work almost every day before rehearsals began and every day during the rehearsal period. That took up about six weeks. Not a lot of time to put together a big show that was also going to be a movie. We recorded the entire show at Capitol Records in Hollywood, mostly in the evenings after rehearsal or during the shooting schedule, so it was a very exhausting and vocally wearing process. The sound engineer and the musical director really wanted as much live singing during the shooting as Bette could do because it had such an honest ring to it while she was actually playing the part. Such hard work.

In the final cut, they did use a lot of her live singing, and I thought that was totally the right thing to do. I believe I was on that project about four months, and I truly enjoyed it. The project was a huge success and Bette and I have been working together ever since. She has done some magnificent singing on her latest albums and in her live shows.

♪

I would not say that my favorite thing to do is work on a movie set or in a recording studio. I love to work on live shows so much more. Recordings and movies are tedious work to someone like me. Too much time sitting in studios while technical work is being done. But I now have an appreciation for both of those art forms that I did not have before. So one is always learning new areas of this business. I have to admit that I always kind of snubbed my nose at people who were recording artists, but oh boy, have I changed my mind about that form of artistry.

During *Gypsy* I met one of the loveliest men. I don't know if it is proper to call a man lovely, but it is the way I will describe Peter Riegert. He was so generous to me. Whenever I needed a place to rest or get away for a few minutes, he offered me his trailer to hang out in. What a blessing that was. It was very hot, and since Peter was not on the set every day, I had someplace to go and relax. I would just tell the stage manager that I would be in Peter's trailer, and they would come and get me when I was needed.

*Peter & Bette*

As Herbie, Peter did have to sing in the movie, so we worked on his parts and the harmonies that he had to do with Bette. I am always so happy to see him when I am in New York or he is in California. A fine actor and a wonderful person. I don't know whether he has sung since that time, but I did think he did a remarkable job. He was a little scared of the singing but it came off quite well.

Many people never knew that Bette and Peter had lived together for a few years back in the '80s. So it was interesting for them to be working closely together on *Gypsy*. Peter handled it very well, and Bette did too after she got through the first couple of days of rehearsal. They were very good together in the show.

You really do become a family on these projects because you are together all day, either working, or eating, or relaxing. One thing that I thought was most amusing was how important food is on a movie set. It seems like that gets the most consideration. Amusing, but also very important that you have food—and lots of it. So one can literally eat all day.

Bette was very particular about the quality of food that was served, and she also had a cappuccino machine set up with someone there to make cappuccinos all day long for everyone. (I believe we went through at least three caterers before everyone was happy and approved of the food.) So my experience on *Gypsy* was a pleasant one.

# ♪ Chapter Twenty-Five ♬

## My New, Wonderful Companion

*"All Mankind Loves a Lover"*
*~Ralph Waldo Emerson*

♪

In 1992, I met Larry and Ann O'Brian at the Saddleback Church of Religious Science in Laguna Hills, California. I had been involved with Religious Science for many years, and for me it was a terrific philosophy for living one's everyday life. This philosophy was created by Dr. Ernest Holmes. The philosophy is actually called Science of Mind and the church is Religious Science. (Not to be confused with Christian Science or Scientology.) Larry and Ann were members of the church and were very active in it. I, on the other hand, was a Sunday-morning-only attendee. Because I had sung for every denomination you can imagine, I did not have a lot of interest in getting too personally involved with any church. Some of you may understand that working for a church is not the same as simply attending it. I had finally retired from that part of my life when I stopped singing in Jewish temples, and the last job of singing that I had was in a Greek Orthodox church. Now that runs the gamut of religious organizations—from Christian Science to Greek Orthodox to Catholic and Jewish temples.

Ann was ill with cancer when I met them, and in December of 1992 she passed away. I was not around too many Sundays during this time because I was finishing the movie with Bette and basically living in Los Angeles. However, toward the end of 1993, just as I was finishing that job, I was at church one Sunday morning and Larry asked me if I would like to go to brunch the next Sunday. I think I had to make it two weeks later, but we did indeed go to brunch. That seemed to clinch the deal and we began to see each other regularly.

The first thing that I realized was that if I was going to be with this man, I had better learn to play golf. That was something that I had been telling myself I was going to do for my hobby when I moved to Laguna Woods but, of course, I had not gotten around to it.

So the first thing Larry bought me was a set of secondhand golf clubs to begin to learn the game. I took a few lessons—not enough, but I

♪

Marge & Larry

started to play with him and it was a good sport for us to do together. To enlighten you about my type A personality, I went to the golf range one day and got a big bucket of balls to practice with. About the third or fourth swing, I felt my back crunch. Do you think I quit hitting those balls? No. So I really injured my back and was in a lot of pain for quite a few weeks.

We had planned a trip to Australia and New Zealand, and I was barely able to walk when we left. I had gone to a sports physical therapy place and had lots of exercises to do, and I did manage to get through that trip. The highlight of the trip was getting to attend two performances at the Sydney Opera House. I had always wanted to see that place, as I had heard that the acoustics were fabulous.

New Zealand is beautiful, and we enjoyed seeing both the south and north islands. Our trip ended with almost a week of relaxation in Fiji. That was truly romantic and restful after so much sightseeing. Larry loved to snorkel, and I loved being in a canoe, so I would follow him around in the canoe while he was snorkeling. Great fun. We met a wonderful Australian couple while in Fiji, and we spent quite a bit of time sitting in the pool bar, meaning we were sitting in the water but on barstools. It was the best.

Larry owned a time-share and so we traded that for lots of vacations and just generally had a wonderful time together. The year after we started seeing each other, we made a trip to New York City. Of course I had to show him off to all my friends and colleagues. My dear friends David Friedman and Scott Barnes threw a fabulous party at their apartment and told me to invite as many people as I wanted to. They did everything. I kept trying to help with something, but they just wanted us to show up and enjoy the evening. We really did, and everybody thought Larry was the greatest. They were so happy for me and approved of my choice.

We took a fabulous trip to Hong Kong, Bangkok and Singapore. Larry really wanted to go to Hong Kong before it reverted back to China, and I agreed to do the trip even though I had never had a huge interest in going to Asia. Well, famous last words. It was one of the loveliest trips I have ever experienced. I felt completely at home in Hong Kong, as it is so much like New York City. I had no problem getting around the city: the subway system is so fantastic and clean that you simply take it everywhere. A wonderful and beautiful revolving restaurant was our choice for our last evening in Hong Kong and it was great.

Bangkok lived up to be much more than I expected, and the highlight for me was being at the Royal Palace, which was the true setting of *The King and I.* Larry was sick that day and so I carried around the video camera plus my still camera and could not stop taking pictures. But you could not possibly capture the opulence and beauty of the buildings that made up the Royal Palace and it was truly beautiful.

In three and a half years we did lots of traveling and playing. Larry loved show business and particularly musical theater, so it was a total joy for us to go together to Broadway shows and to theater in general. He also liked to accompany me when I was giving voice lessons in the Los Angeles area. Wherever I was teaching, he would take a book and sit and read. The first time Dixie Carter met him, she was taken aback at how much he looked like her husband, Hal Holbrook. A nice compliment.

I met Dixie Carter in Los Angeles in 1994. She had just about given up singing. She had been a singer all her life, taking voice lessons from a very young age in Tennessee. Later in New York City, she had a wonderful teacher by the name of Robley Lawson. She was trained in opera and classical music and also took piano lessons. She is quite an accomplished musician. This was also during the time of *Designing Women* and she was using her speaking voice a lot in her role.

Having encountered some vocal challenges, she had been seeing a voice teacher in Los Angeles for some time but had not seen any improvement, even though she was a dedicated and hard-working student. As I recall, what she told me was that she asked the voice teacher to discuss with her where she was going with this technique. The teacher hesitated and finally said to her, "Maybe it's just over for you." Imagine how Dixie felt hearing someone she trusted say that to her! She didn't sing for months, and then she had a call from a fine pianist and arranger, Mike Renzi in New York, who told her about me and that I was living in Southern California. She called. We got together and have been working together ever since. Dixie continues to do her cabaret shows in New York and elsewhere, and was brilliant in the Broadway production of *Master Class*. It was not "over" for her.

# ♪ Chapter Twenty-Six ♫

## Reasons for Teaching

*"Either you reach a higher point today,
or you exercise your strength in order
to be able to climb higher tomorrow"*
*~Friedrich Nietzsche*

♪

Larry passed away in 1997. It was a real shock. There I was again, starting life anew by myself. Not quite by myself, as his family had adopted me and so I gained a wonderful group to continue on with. But it was so hard to lose him. As time went on, some people again suggested that I start writing this book, and this time I felt it was the appropriate time to accomplish this task—and task it was. Getting back to teaching certainly helped, and since I was taking the time and contemplating my work, I wanted to begin here to include my findings and beliefs in the "how to's" of my teaching.

I truly believe that there are people who are meant to be teachers or instructors and there are people who should not ever attempt to teach. Knowing something and teaching it are two entirely different things. For example, when Larry was trying to teach me to use the computer, it was a total disaster. I said to him all the time that you cannot teach someone by doing it for them. You have to have the patience and ability to explain over and over again the process and then let the student do the work. I don't think I ever reached him with that idea. He was so quick and I was so slow.

So the first ingredient for a teacher is patience with a capital P. For some unknown reason, I have all the patience in the world for teaching, explaining, and going over and over something without getting the least bit irritated or frustrated. This is a quality that has served me so well. But I want you to understand that I am a person who has "zilch" patience in life, as many of my friends would tell you. So where I received this quality from is still a mystery to me. I guess God gave me the ability to understand what that quality meant in teaching and generously gave it to me.

I am also a firm believer in facing yourself honestly and knowing what your motives are in becoming a teacher. Particularly a voice or acting teacher. What are your true feelings about your students? Is it that you want them to succeed where maybe you feel you did not succeed? It is so important to know your own feelings and motives.

Money is a large consideration for everyone. But if money is the main motive, I do not believe you can give your students all the personal attention and support that they need. I have known too many teachers who give half-hour lessons and go strictly by the hands on the clock. Stopping a student in the middle of a phrase or song is very rude and debilitating to the student's sense of importance. Do you, as the teacher, truly want your students to succeed and achieve more success than you were able to achieve? This is a tough question and one that, I believe, must be answered honestly. Only after you have put to rest your own personal desires and disappointments are you ready to give your students your undivided attention and loyalty.

Now, what are you going to give your students that will benefit them in their chosen field? First, you must look at the student honestly. That means, however, with no judgment. I can't tell you how many times I have been wrong in my evaluation of what I thought a particular student could accomplish. First, their desire is the strongest indicator. Second is discipline. Third is talent. Sometimes the most talented people are not disciplined enough to move into big careers. The disciplined student can rise to the best use of their talents and that sometimes moves them further along than the very talented person. The desire to be active and working in your chosen field is one of the strongest motivations one can have. So, in teaching a new student, be careful not to judge too quickly what that student will be able to accomplish.

Love of teaching must be present at all times. Remind yourself that the love of teaching is why you are doing it. All the other things, like success and money and recognition, come from that love.

At one time I asked a very talented young singer why she was trying to make a career in the theater. Her answer was, "Because I want to be a star." Wrong motivation and certainly the wrong answer in *my* studio. You want to be in the theater because you love it. It's your passion. Again, the other things will follow or not, but the love of the art is the thing. You strive to always do your best and be prepared for that moment when success just might land in your lap.

The story of Shirley MacLaine is one of the perfect examples of what can happen to an understudy. Her break was the result of another actress's bad luck. In 1954, MacLaine was understudy to Broadway actress Carol Haney in *Pajama Game*. Haney fractured her ankle. MacLaine replaced her and was spotted and offered a movie contract by producer Hal Wallis. It affirms how you should always do your best work, even though you are not the star of the show.

# ♪ Chapter Twenty-Seven ♫

## Teaching a New Student

*"There is a vitality, a life force, a quickening that is translated through you into action, and because there is only one of you in all time, this expression is unique"*
~Martha Graham to Agnes De Mille

# Marge Rivingston

♪

Since singing involves the whole body, just as dance does, singers should know their own bodies intimately and how their bodies support their singing voice. I have found it easy to work with dancers who want to be able to sing, because they understand the body connection so well. Warming up the body certainly helps the process of warming up the voice. Warming up the body also helps to relieve nervous tension and relaxes the muscles so that the singing is freer and the voice more open. Too many singers do not put enough importance on the connection between the whole body and the voice.

I remember Linda Ronstadt telling me after she had sung with Placido Domingo that she could feel vibration coming through his entire body when he was singing. She said it was amazing to stand next to him and feel that sound vibrating throughout his whole body. When supporting a voice like he has, it is true that the whole body vibrates with the sound. After singing a duet with him, she said she thought she should change careers and be a shoe salesman. I told her I was glad she didn't make that decision.

Now we come to understanding the function of the breath. I think this has always been a nebulous part of teaching voice, and hard for most students to understand. The importance of the usage of the breath *is* what I am talking about. Students are told, all too often, to take a deep breath, expand the diaphragm and the back and then sing. Now most of that idea is okay except for the fact that most people do not know what the diaphragm actually does. It is really a very lazy muscle. Only if you keep telling it to work for you will it begin to develop the strength that it needs to support the voice.

As the voice develops more sound and power, I have found that the student feels that they do not have as much breath as they need for a phrase. So that is where the diaphragm comes into play. The voice mechanism will develop more quickly than the breath support from the diaphragm, so that the student feels they run out of breath while singing. Now the diaphragm, being innately lazy, doesn't want to have to work harder to support this person's voice. So what do we do?

The diaphragm will do the work, but not without direction and concentration. We keep informing it that we need more air, and slowly it will supply us with the air we need to support the sound. So, it is a game between the development of the voice and the breath control to support that voice. And it *is* a game. One moves and then the other has to catch up. Sounds like a lot of fun, doesn't it?

Do not panic because you don't possess all the air you want in the beginning of developing your voice. Do not tense up and try to sing longer phrases than you are capable of supporting, because you will simply use tension to do this. Figure out places within a phrase where you can breathe easily and naturally, and no one will even know you are doing it if you can incorporate the extra breath into your interpretation of the lyric. What I want to emphasize right now is using the breath you have at the moment and using it efficiently.

One of the words that I would like to see disappear from voice teaching is the word "control." That word suggests "holding" and that is the last thing you want to do in singing. Do not hold your breath in. Breath is always moving and not being held. The concept of that moving sound is very important so as not to develop tensions in the throat or in the diaphragm. There is an old idea of thinking of breathing in and out like the old "bellows" that were used to fan fires. Also, sort of like an accordion movement. So the breath goes in, but it also comes out with the sound. Then, if you get into the rhythm of this idea of moving breath, you will find it easier to take in the new breath if you have released most of the old breath. Feel the breath going in and out and producing the sound on top of that exhale. Keep it all moving.

We have touched on diaphragmatic breathing and the movement of sound. Now what about the word "resonance"? Reading the meaning of the word "resonance" in the dictionary was an astounding revelation for me. It explained what I believe about resonance being such an important part of the whole function of vocal sound. Here is what it says: "prolongation of sound by reflection—reverberation." Prolongation would mean moving tone or sound. It certainly does reverberate, and that again is

♪

continuation of sound.

Then there is "amplification of a source of speech sounds, especially in the cavities of phonation by sympathetic vibration of the air, especially in the cavities of the mouth, nose and pharynx." The dictionary also says that "resonance is a characteristic quality of a particular voice speech sound imparted by the distribution of amplitudes among the cavities of the head, chest and throat." It goes on to say that "a larger than normal vibration is produced in response to a stimulus whose frequency is close to the natural frequency of the vibrating system." It ends with "a quality of enriched significance, profundity or allusiveness. Such as the poem has a resonance beyond its surface meaning. To resound!" Wow, that explains resonance pretty well for me. Now this definition is talking about speech, but just think how much more important these vibratory sensations are in singing. I rest my case for the importance of true resonance being part of singing technique.

Now, by adding one of my favorite words—"placement"—to this discussion, we are beginning to get a picture of my ideas of a singing technique. Placement involves some other thoughts and ideas. What do teachers mean when they refer to placement? My definition of vocal placement is "where you feel the sound being produced from." Or vibrating from. Is it being produced forward in the mouth or back further in the throat? Where are the sensations coming from? What makes the sound bright or dark? What makes a sound nasal or simply resonant? What do the vocal cords actually do to produce sound? What other muscles are involved in producing sound and volume? These are only a few of the questions that need to be answered so that a student understands what the individual voice is capable of producing.

This is how I treat a new or prospective student when they come into my studio. First, I usually ask them what their background is in singing, how long they have been singing, what type of training they have had in high school or college, and what their favorite type of music is. Then I ask what they think I can do for them, and what they think we can accomplish together for them in their individual development. After this conversation, which might take ten or fifteen minutes of their lesson time, I ask them if they would like me to warm them up with a few introductory exercises of mine or if they would simply like to sing a song for me. I think the response has always been equally divided between the two choices. Usually, after I hear either a little rudimentary exercise or one song, I can pinpoint what the vocal development or problem is.

I don't really know why I have the ability or talent to diagnose a voice almost immediately, but I believe it has to do, in part, with having a lot of years of teaching and doing vocal therapy work. However, I also believe that some teachers have an innate ability to know what is stopping the student from being able to realize their true vocal power. This sounds a bit like the mystic, but I do believe that one can tune into the student's blocks and know how to unlock those blocks—be they emotional, psychological, or just plain fear of failure. Trial and error have taught me how to handle most of these vocal problems or to know intuitively how to help the student overcome any vocal difficulties. The other side of this coin is how easy it is when you, as a teacher, get a fresh voice that has not been tampered with.

The range of the voice also comes into this diagnosis. How do you develop more range of sound from top to bottom? I firmly believe that you must exercise/vocalize the entire instrument. Some teachers teach that singing is an extension of the speaking voice. I don't disagree with this theory, but I do not believe that it goes far enough in developing a rich and powerful singing tone.

After informing the prospective student what I think their vocal problems are and how I would approach dealing with these problems, I always try to emphasize what I believe at the moment are the good and strong points about their singing. So often the technique has been so "phonied up" that it is hard to tell what the true voice would sound like.

But singing should not be hard work! Yes, it is physically challenging and singers must be in optimum physical condition in order to get the very best sound out of their instrument—the physical body. We do not have a large instrument like the piano or the bass fiddle to depend on to produce this sound. We produce it from our own body.

So, if a person decides to study with me, we get right to work. Occasionally I know that I get too excited with a new student and give them a little too much to absorb in the beginning, but that is my type A personality. Usually it works really well and the students love getting new ideas immediately to work with on their own. I also firmly believe that the teacher is only the guiding hand to give students ideas to develop their own unique talents and gifts. The teacher must understand that students need to know their own voice and how to use it and also how to treat it. Sometimes students tend to abuse their instrument and not know how to treat it with gentleness and kindness. It is such a great communicator and needs to be treated with total respect.

The technique that I try to give my students is one that they can take and make their own and know how to fix any problems that may arise from time to time—for example, illness, fatigue, jet lag, or allergies. How does one handle these things when one is on the road and doing eight shows a week?

And not only eight shows a week, but at one point, the Broadway producers—God love them—decided to do what we now call a five-show weekend. So on Friday night you start your five back-to-back shows. By Sunday night the cast is exhausted. Then, if you are in a road company or on a bus and truck tour, consider that you may be moving the next day and opening another city the day after. Extra rehearsals are tucked in there too. A killer schedule. When do the body and the voice get a rest? You need to be really strong in your vocal technique to handle this type of schedule.

This reminds me of a couple of talented musicians who came to study with me. One is a well-known bass player, Jay Leonhart, and a reed player, Lou Marini. The best! They were both tops in their field, but they loved to sing and wanted to improve their voices and abilities as vocalists. I gave them some exercises that I thought would help build their voices, and when they came in for other lessons, both of them had totally changed my exercises to suit what they thought they needed. I loved it. The creativity was really showing and it was great. They were both still accomplishing the necessary connections between breath and sound that I was trying to get them to develop.

Getting into another vocal technique misconception, I would like to touch on the idea of always singing with a so-called "low larynx." There are a lot of different opinions relating to this idea. Many teachers are adamant about keeping the larynx low, or down. To my mind this is simply a way to get the student hooked into an idea that they can get only from this particular teacher. And also, since it is pretty impossible to attain that state throughout a lot of singing, I think it simply makes the student crazy and believing that they are not able to accomplish what the teacher is asking them to do. Not a very encouraging way to work.

I myself do not believe in "pressing" the larynx down. I think it lowers the tongue too much in the back of the throat and makes the tone darker and further back than I think is healthy. There, I've said it! It also jams the hyoid bone down to the larynx and so destroys the movability of the whole mechanism. It seems to make sense to me that if you—now follow this—push the back of the tongue down to lower the larynx, you are also tightening the muscles that surround the vocal cords, or more accurately, the vocal folds. Picture it. The tongue is connected to the voice box and the muscles surrounding the cords. So if you hold the back of the tongue down, the muscles will tighten and the cords will have a harder time vibrating the pitch you want. They will try to make the fabulous pitch that you are hearing in your ear, but you are putting undue pressure on them, and they get tired of having to work so hard to produce the "perfect tone." Too much concentration on the "low" larynx stops the student from being free with their sound and expression.

# ♪ Chapter Twenty-Eight ♫

## Musical Directors and Learning New Material

*"The most perfect technique
is that which is not noticed at all"
~Pablo Casals*

This brings me to the times when I have fought with musical directors over how they teach new songs to a performer. Say it is a new show, has never been done before, and the music has to be learned from scratch. So the "brilliant" music director—and I mean that sincerely—plays the piece through for the performer and then wants the performer to stand up and sing it. Pretty ridiculous. And usually, they want it up to tempo too. What I have always tried to do is explain to the musical director that the voice needs time and work to be comfortable with new material. To start out slowly through the musical phrases. Then, how about the tempo or timing? Not everyone these days knows what the length of a thirty-second note is or, for that matter, how many beats there are in a measure of music. So I have tried to explain that the voice needs to go through this process of learning.

Here is my list of rules as to how a piece of new music should be learned: First learn the melody. Then the timing (fast or slow). Then the words. And the last thing to put into the song is the expression or the interpretation of the lyrics. Now you have a whole picture of a piece of music, and the voice is totally comfortable with expressing it. Equate this process again with that of a dancer. How long and arduous is the training of the muscles to do a new ballet? As a singer, we are dealing with a set of muscles, and they need to be trained for each new piece of music.

There is one other thing to be considered: the key in which the piece will be performed. In the days of Richard Rodgers and Oscar Hammerstein, there was no choice of keys. In their musicals, the performer had to perform the songs in the keys that they were written in. Richard Rodgers was very specific about why he insisted on the original keys. He explained that he wrote the entire score so that each song would flow into the next one with the feeling or the mood that he was trying to accomplish and not be repetitive in the keys they were sung in. Hard for us to understand exactly what he meant, but the entire score had a pattern to it of movement and sound so that it was complete in itself. I am sure Stephen Sondheim would agree and explain it better than I have.

There is always so little rehearsal time allotted to this important job, that everything gets rushed. So if you do read music, you are way ahead of the game. I always encourage young people to take some piano lessons or sight-singing classes, which help you to read the music and understand it much more quickly.

I believe that a lot of the time you never hear the music sung as well as it could be because of the lack of proper processing and rehearsal. You can also imagine how the breathing apparatus responds to this quick, quick, quick, get-it-done attitude. Where is the beauty of sound in all this? Some people can do the work on their own or with their teacher, and some people don't have that luxury or can't afford to pay for those lessons. This coaching is not available to them.

There is a difference between a voice teacher and a voice coach. I have been called both, but I always try to make it clear that I am a voice teacher first—that I do coach people on their songs, musically and interpretively, but I prefer to leave that part of the training to a good vocal coach. Basically, a vocal coach works on the musical phrasing and presentation of the song, whereas I work on the vocal placement and vocal comfort of the key.

As a vocal instructor, what am I really working with to create beautiful singing? We do not have a big, massive piece of wood like a piano, with its own sounding board and tuning ability. Nor a violin, cello or any other stringed instrument to tune up and play. We have to rely on our bodies to produce the entire spectrum of beautiful sound. That is why basic good health is so important for the singer. Then the breath flowing to bring the tone out for us to hear, and the resonance for the sound to carry out into the theater.

The sinus resonators, the mouth resonation on the hard palate, and the chest resonance make up how the sound becomes beautiful. There are other slight variations on the placement, but that needs to be done with a teacher and on the spot. I am trying to give you, the student or teacher, the basic beliefs I have about the art of the singing technique. I want to emphasize again that I believe with all my heart that singing should be joyous, full of individual expression, and easy. Now, "easy" means that you have done all the work necessary to make it easy. The development over a period of time to realize the potential of your unique instrument. That does take time and work, but it must be the right kind of work.

# ♪ Chapter Twenty-Nine ♫

## Catching Up and
## New Adventures

*"Above all, do not despair when the hand*
*of criticism plunges into your body and claws at your soul.*
*You must endure it, accept it and smile.*
*It is your life and your choice."*
*~Sir Laurence Olivier*

♪

Marge & Bette

Catching up with some of my performers, I was on the road for most of 2004 and 2005. First with Bette Midler when she was doing her tour called *Kiss My Brass*. It was a great show, and she is such a brilliant performer. Everything from the funniest to the most heartfelt singing. She demands so much from her voice and body that it is extremely hard work. But how the audiences respond is quite incredible. So my function there was to travel with her and the company a lot of the time and warm her up for each show. Sometimes she really did not want to do it, but she knew that she needed to in order to stay in top vocal condition for the tour. She also ran on the treadmill every day, and I occasionally watched her. How amazing! She built up so much stamina, and it also warmed up the body so that her singing was freer when she started warming up. It was a great experience for me, and the whole company was terrific.

Linda & Marge

Bette is so generous with her entire company, and we all came away with a beautiful suitcase, jacket and vest—all with *Kiss My Brass* on them.

During part of this time I was also on the road with Linda Ronstadt. What a pleasure that is to hear her sing every night. Such a beautiful voice and great interpretation of standard tunes. Again, my function was to warm her up every day, attend the show, and make any notes for the next

140

day. It was a beautiful tour with great musicians. We also had part of the Boston Symphony Orchestra traveling with us most of the time, so her show encompassed a lot of different styles of music.

Then there was Maureen McGovern who was on the road with the musical version of *Little Women*. (She loves to do a Broadway show and have the opportunity to do more acting as well as singing.) Now, Maureen was very dedicated, and different, in the sense that she would never think of going onstage without a vocal warm-up. We managed to get one voice lesson in before she went out for a year on the road.

The great thing for me now is that I am free to be out on the road when needed. Semiretired and without a huge clientele, I can easily get away for weeks at a time. Never could have done that in New York.

After making the move back to California, I really had no idea what my teaching life would be like. I trusted that there were people here who would want and need what I had to offer as a teacher. That proved to be true.

As I remember, it was in the summer of 1999 that Maureen McGovern was hired for two jazz concerts in Utah. A singer by the name of Jack Wood was to be her opening act. He found out that Maureen studied with me and he wanted a lesson with me before the concerts. Jack is a very fine singer and well-known in Utah and here in Orange County. He is a true lover of the "great American songbook" and sings all those tunes beautifully. We have continued to work together these ensuing years.

Through Jack, many of the local jazz performers have come to work vocally with me. I say that one is never too old to learn new things, and I have learned so much from all these performers. Mainly, to appreciate the love these artists have for the art of jazz. Musically it is a very challenging art form. In teaching these artists, it is really about having a good technique and then using it in any form of music that you love.

In 2001, through Jack, I had the extreme pleasure of going to Salt Lake City to conduct a vocal master class during their annual jazz festival. This four-day festival is held the weekend after July 4 and has continued to be a yearly highlight in my schedule. It is a joy to work with the young people there and encourage them to pursue their talents. We have the best time, and I am so privileged to be included in the long jazz festival

weekend. It is a free festival for everyone in the area and is well attended each year. Lots of good singers, inspiring musicians, and a great time to be in that beautiful city.

*Master Class*

# ♪ Chapter Thirty ♫

## My Personal Philosophy

*"Our word is what creates our world.*
*Keeping our word is what makes our world work"*
*~David Friedman, Musician - Composer*

♪

At this point I want to write about my philosophy of life and how to achieve some of the dreams and visions that people have inside them. Whether rich or poor or just in between, individuals have the potential to accomplish one or more of their dreams. I am always amazed by people saying they are bored with life. How can that possibly be true? There is so much to do, to see, to experience. I will never have the energy or the years to see and do everything my heart would like to do. But I am going to do as many of those things as I possibly can while I am here on this beautiful planet.

Experiencing other cultures and other countries and their unique beauties has been a wonderful and satisfying experience for me. I believe that the old adage "travel broadens one's mind" is very true. To see the diversity and the sameness of our human race is truly eye-opening.

Are you brave enough to open your eyes and your heart to know what you want for your own life? It seems like a simple question, but in my experience I have found that the majority of people are too afraid to take the risks involved in finding out what they really want out of their life. I read somewhere recently that we have made people fit into the mold of available jobs and never thought to make the jobs fit into the people's abilities and desires.

Desire is not a selfish thing. Get that straight right now. No artist in any medium would ever accomplish their desire if they really thought it was pure selfishness. We would not have the museums and art galleries without those people with their vision and their talent and the willingness to get out there and try. It's like the old joke that goes "How do you get to Carnegie Hall? Practice, practice, practice." This does not mean that you will get to Carnegie Hall, but you will get to some other hall and you will realize a great deal of your dream.

Or, let's say that you want to be a "Broadway baby." How do you get to Broadway? I could give you a lot of answers, but one of the simplest would be to get yourself to New York City. Now, to most people that would mean stopping their dream right there. Too much risk involved.

But you don't have to be a "Broadway baby" to be a musical

theater performer. There are many outlets for that in other places in the country, but why not set your sights on the very biggest and best avenue for that expression.

Often I have observed that young people are held back by their parents' fears. Leaving home and going to the "big bad city" is just too frightening for parents to encourage or support their child in that dream. My thoughts are that if you don't do it when you are young and have the ambition and the drive to experience your dream, you will never do it. There is plenty of time to direct your life differently if it doesn't work out in New York City. It really isn't that scary and you sure figure out whether you want to pursue that particular goal. But try it first.

I remember having a conversation with my father after I had been somewhat successful in New York. He told me that he had always been very happy and contented being a big fish in a little pond. That perfectly described Santa Ana, California, to me. So I said to him that I had to attempt to be a big fish in a big pond and that was New York City to me. I do not regret one day that I spent in that magnificent city or my work there. You grow up quickly. There are definitely scary and lonely moments in this way of living, but when your heart and mind are driven to that place, you really have no choice but to honor that desire.

Because of individual life circumstances, not all people have the opportunity to explore this option, but your path can veer off in another direction and you will still accomplish a big part of your dream—wherever you are.

If going to New York City sounds and feels right to you, it means dedicating your life to your chosen field. New York is a tough city. It does not care whether you make it or not. There are plenty of other people to take your place. It is impossible to be dishonest with yourself in that city. It demands that you look at yourself very honestly and decide whether you can take all the knocks the City is liable to hand out to you. But, on the other side of that coin is the joy of meeting all the people who are going through the same undertaking and catharsis that you are and sharing your life with them. You become a very large family in a very large city and

♪

that is your protection.

It is interesting to me that when you put yourself out there, you will always meet like-minded people. Sometimes in our society, it seems that show people are looked down on and that they are labeled as self-indulgent, lazy, nonproductive individuals. Oh boy, does that rile me up. Starving and striving for that acceptance of your talent is one of the most worthy ambitions I can think of. To love your dream so passionately—to live a very fulfilling and rich life. No one can take that away from you and no one can fire you for it. You own your own soul and that is a life worth living.

Maybe I am still a dreamer, but I wish for each and every one of you the guts that I know it takes to stick to your dream or vision. Life can throw you many curves, but you don't have to let them discourage you. Stop, listen, and then make your own decision as to what is right for you. Try not to listen to too many people or to get too many opinions, because it will only confuse you. You can get side-tracked from your dream, but you don't have to give up the dream. There are many roads to take that will give your dream a place to live and work.

This does not mean that every one of you can chuck it all and move to New York. So work with where you are and what you can do—and enjoy doing it. You never know where it will lead you. If you do nothing to follow your dream, I'm sure all of you know what will happen. Absolutely nothing. So move and keep moving until something that lightens your heart and makes you sing comes through. I know it will happen that way.

These thoughts bring me to mention the presence of a Higher Power guiding our lives. I am not talking about religion. I am talking about trust in a Universe that will support you in your endeavors. Do you trust the Universe to support you in your vision for your life's work? Do you believe that you can have all the good that you envision? Tough questions! No easy answers. My belief is that the trust you have in the Universe to provide for you helps you get through the rejections and hard paths of this business. To have a strong belief in yourself as part of an orderly and loving Universe allows you to continue to move toward your chosen goal.

I can only impart to all of you what I believe has helped me achieve my personal success with the people I have been privileged to know and work with. They have all given me a wonderful life to live and to share with the many people I have encountered and continue to encounter in this ongoing understanding of how "life works."

It seems to be very difficult to end this book, but I want to leave you with some quotations from Dr. Ernest Holmes. Holmes says that "true teaching liberates the student from the teacher. One will find the teacher within oneself." I love that quotation and it has been my belief as a teacher.

He goes on to say, "Use your talent to create a greater expression of life. You should have a spirit of adventure in this—the wonder of it, the continual discovery, the steady unfoldment, the joyful anticipation of more and better. The recognition of one's partnership with the Universe." And so it is!

**\*\***

# ♪ APPENDIX I ♫

## Vocal Exercises

♪

So, how does a student begin to develop his or her instrument? Some people believe in doing breathing exercises. I think that is okay if you feel it strengthens the diaphragm and gives you more breath. But my belief is, for a singer, you must connect the breath with some singing sound in order for that connection to be built into the technique and for the use of economy in releasing the breath.

At this time I am going to include my explanation of beginning exercises, all of which are included on the CD that accompanies this book. Demonstrations are done by both a female and a male vocalist. I think it is the most efficient way of hearing and feeling what I teach as far as building a technique.

## WARM-UP EXERCISES

No. 1 - I usually start out with what I call a "yawn\sigh" exercise. That means that you start by opening the jaw and mouth space and sighing the breath out over an octave, such as middle G to low G. Then you breathe in again and repeat the sigh over an octave drop, moving up by half steps using the vowel "oo" and sliding down opening to "ah" at the low note. You are stretching the membranes of the palate and the mouth space—releasing the jaw and generally stretching out the muscles inside the throat and mouth. Depending on the ability and range of the singer, I will take this exercise up to a high B-flat if it is possible. Otherwise, just stretch the range as far as it is comfortable, and you will find that after a few weeks you will be able to stretch the palate more and reach another step or two. All of these exercises apply to men as well as to women. The male voice will float into the falsetto and that is the right way to warm up the male instrument.

This exercise is simply to get the breath, space and tone all working simultaneously without any pressure on the kind of sound you are making. The teachers who want to hear nothing but beautiful sounds out of a student right in the beginning make no sense to me at all. You must stretch all those intrinsic muscles the same way dancers would do their barre before attempting to dance a difficult role. Why we have this idea that singing is a natural talent, I don't know. The quality of the voice will show itself later on with the development of the instrument, and then the decision will be made as to the God-given quality of that particular instrument. In the meantime, do the work and build the technique and wait for the final judgment to be made.

No. 2 - I decided to include another beginning exercise so that you, as the student or teacher, can decide which one opens the voice up in the best way. This exercise starts out using the vowel "oo" (pronounced "who"), descending four notes and opening to "ah" on the fifth note. Starting at G above middle C and descending to middle C. Go on down to about a D to G range. Then start in the middle again and go up with the same five-note scale to around a C above middle C to high G. This is all explained on the CD. Remember to relax the tongue forward as you open the "ah" vowel.

No. 3 - So, the next thing we want to do is loosen up all of the tongue muscles and get them very agile. Particularly the back of the tongue. It should be lying relaxed in the back, not raised up or lowered down with a muscle action. Just open your mouth, drop your jaw, keep the tongue lightly against the bottom teeth and see how relaxed your tongue is. That is the ultimate position for the tongue to return to after singing words.

The tongue also has to be free in order to accomplish a fast patter song, such as Stephen Sondheim's "Another Hundred People." Talk about difficult pieces to negotiate both vocally and in enunciation! Another one of his would be "I'm Not Getting Married Today." Both of these numbers are from *Company*, and when he wrote them, he must have been in a mood to make female singers really have to work. Try one of them sometime and see if you can figure out how to even get a breath in somehow or somewhere.

So a little exercise I developed for the loosening of the tongue is called "kiddily kit." Don't ask how I thought this one up. It just came to me when someone needed to loosen the tongue and move through a fast passage of a song. I do it fast on a triad like Bb-D-F-D-Bb. So "kiddily" is on Bb-D-F-D-Bb, and "kit" is on Bb. Fun, huh? This little exercise is done up the scale by half steps. It loosens the back and front of the tongue and places the tone quite forward. Don't go above about a high F, meaning an octave and a fourth above middle C. It will tend to tighten the throat a little if you take it too high. It is not as easy as it appears to be when you try to keep getting it faster. Many people cannot loosen the tongue that quickly. Also remember to keep a little air moving through the exercise so it does not become tight in the throat.

Next—and let me interject a rule of mine here—be sure to take breaks between exercises. Nowadays, with tapes and CDs being made by most teachers, the tendency is to continue the tape or CD until it is finished. NO, NO, NO. Take little breaks between each exercise. Get a glass of water or a cup of tea, walk around, stretch out the body, and then do the next exercise. You will find that the voice is able to build more strength and stamina this way. This time-out allows the muscles to relax.

Now, I don't mean to make phone calls on these minibreaks. Talking on the phone is one of the most tiring things the voice has to put up with. I believe it is because we are so eager to get our point across to the person on the other end of the line that we press too hard and probably speak too forcefully. So the minibreak is not for that kind of activity. So, if a vocalizing tape is twenty minutes long, it should take you, the student, at least thirty or forty minutes to finish your vocal warm-up.

No. 4 - In the next exercise, I insert some light staccato work. You start on a G above middle C and do four staccatos on an "oo" vowel and then on the fifth note do an "ah." Come down a five-note major scale legato, or smoothly, to middle C on the "ah." Hopefully, most of you will know what a major scale is, but you will hear all of these on the CD, so that will help you understand the notes. An example of a major scale consists of one octave starting at middle C and moving from C-D-E-F-G-A-B-C. What I want here is the explanation of what the exercise accomplishes for you in your technique work. For the male voice, you simply start most of the exercises the octave below where the female starts. So in this case, the male voice would start on the G below middle C and continue the same way.

Now, the staccatos should be done from the diaphragm and not from the throat. Tricky! The diaphragm should be pulled in on the first staccato, not pushed out. So on the four staccatos you are pulling in the diaphragm on each one, then relaxing it on the "ah" and coming down smoothly with a connected legato sound.

The "oo" vowel is a closed sound such as in the word "who." It is not an "oh." This exercise should start in the middle range and go down by half steps into the lower range. (I prefer half steps to whole steps as I believe it helps with intonation.) Then start again in the middle and go up as high as is comfortable. I generally take the female voice to a G above the staff to cover the so-called "bridge," or "passaggio," area. The male voice can go that high if it is not strained. The male voice can lighten up and use more falsetto up that high and warm up the instrument that way instead of yelling full voice. (Oops, did not mean to imply that any singer yells!)

Now we have stretched the mouth and throat and started the breath moving. Also we have loosened the tongue and, last, gotten the diaphragm involved in producing vocal sound. So where do we go next?

Some of you are probably ready to quit right now, but hang on. There is more fun stuff to do with your voice. We are not just going to do boring scales up and down and vowel work. Yes, that is important, but I have found over the years that the musical student already has the ability to make phrases and to sing with good musical sense, so why spend too much time on this area. Later on, the job of phrasing and musicality in songs should be shared with a good vocal coach who works with you on the interpretation of the songs and material that you will be singing. I like building the sound to the place that the student or professional singer can use their own sound in the way that pleases them and have lots of choices in the material that they can sing and perform.

♪

No. 5 - So on to the next vocal exercise. I usually do a four-note scale up and down on a "mee-meh-mah-moh-mee-meh-moo." Simple? Yes. The idea is to get the placement forward in the mouth by using the "m" consonant. So, on C-D-E-F-E-D-C, you sing "mee-meh-mah-moh-mee-meh-moo." Just make sure that the sound has a slight buzz in the mouth and you will be on the right track. Do this exercise slowly from note to note.

These exercises can be used for speech as well as singing. Remember my telling you about working with Natalia Makarova? She did most of these on her speaking voice as that helped her feel where and how she could project her voice. I believe you get more support, extension, range and resonance if you do them with a singing voice, but they are still extremely valuable warm-ups for the actor.

Back to the exercise and starting with the "mee-meh-mah-moh-mee-meh-moo" around E above middle C gives you a chance to then move by half steps down into the lower register. Always keep in mind that the resonance and placement stay forward in the mouth. So go down as low as is comfortable, say to G below middle C, and then starting in the middle again at E, go up by half steps. As you reach the bridge, or passaggio, area, the sound will begin to feel like it wants to go back closer to the soft palate. Allow the soft palate to lift a little (like a slight yawn) and let the tone float up into that soft palate area. The soft palate is a membrane that will stretch, and you want to place your high notes there. You will always know where they are and what they feel like if you can use this placement. Go up to around an F above the staff and that should give you the feeling you are looking to experience.

I have found that some singers don't actually know what or where the soft palate is. And since they don't want to appear stupid, they don't ask. So I will tell you and then you won't have to ask.

The soft palate is an opening that comes from the sinuses and where you sometimes feel a nasal drip coming down into the back of the throat. It is a passageway into vibrating sound for the extremely high notes. We are talking about the tenor voice, the lyric soprano and the coloratura soprano voice.

When asked by a tenor at one of his lessons how to place and sing a high B-flat, one much respected voice teacher replied, "Any way you can." Now that is not very helpful advice to the student, but it does have some truth in it.

I have my own pet theory about how you sing so-called "high notes." My thoughts and experiences with teaching both men and women to be comfortable singing high notes is to explain to them that the place where high notes feel they are being sung from is in that soft palate area. When a student can feel where that sound is being produced, it is actually simpler than the placement of the rest of the voice. The soft palate is a very narrow and vertical passageway, so when you can plug into that space, it is quite easy to sing high notes. And to sing them consistently well. This is a simple method and I have had wonderful success with making singing as easy a process as it can be.

No. 6 - One of the exercises I use is on the vowels "ee-oo." Again, the "oo" is like the word "who." It actually comes out sounding more like "ee-you," which is okay. "Y's" are very useful in getting the sound out of the throat. And this is really a great warming-up exercise. So, starting around F above middle C, on one tone, you simply sing back and forth "ee-oo-ee-oo-ee-oo-ee-oo-ee," holding out the last "ee" to feel the resonance of the sound. Move the mouth back and forth for the wide "ee" and narrow the mouth for the "oo" vowel. What you eventually want to be able to do is keep the tongue absolutely quiet and simply move the mouth for the change of vowels. Start this exercise in the middle, say at F above middle C. Moving by half steps again, because I like them, down to only about B-flat or A and keeping the resonance of the "ee" vowel always in mind. Again, going up from the middle note, move by half steps to about D or E-flat at the top of the staff. Not too high. The "ee" vowel can become tight if taken up too high and not modified a little. This is learning to isolate the tongue movement from the mouth and jaw and allowing them to be independent of one another. Otherwise, I feel that ten years down the line the singer will find himself or herself with myriad vocal problems and no idea how to fix them.

No. 7 - So in keeping with my idea of isolating the muscles, the next exercise I do goes like this (again, the exercise has many variations, but for now we are dealing with the simple version of all my exercises): This one is the opposite of the "ee-oo" in that you are now using the tongue to loosen any tension that might be in the back of the tongue, which attaches to the larynx, or voice box. The tongue is a very strong muscle and on the one hand can help you sustain a note, but on the other hand will create tensions that I *do not* approve of for good singing technique. The reason is that this tension has an effect on the length of your singing career. Tongue tension has no place in a good technique. Basically, the tongue has one function in singing—the function of making consonants so that your words can be understood.

Now for the exercise itself. It is done on the vowels "eh-ah." The jaw is quite open—not to the point of pain, but to the point of opening the hinges of the jaw that are up by the ears. You want to feel space between the bones there, and by dropping the jaw down you should be able to feel some open space. If you can't feel that space, try jutting the chin forward and then dropping the jaw and I think you will feel the space I am refer-ring to. Now the jaw is open and you simply sing "eh-ah," raising the tongue in the back for the "eh" and dropping it for the "ah." The notes are C-D-E-F-G-F-E-D-C. So, up five notes (a major scale) and down to the original note. You have "eh" on the first note, then move up to the second note and sing "ah." Alternate "eh" and "ah" in this manner up and down, ending on "eh" at the bottom note. Now go down by half steps to around a G or F below middle C. After that, go back to the original middle C and go up by half steps through the middle voice and into the top register. The main idea here is to keep the jaw quiet and not moving while you exercise the tongue up and down in the back of the throat. REMEMBER THIS! The tongue is lying relaxed against the bottom teeth. Sometimes it is a good idea to put your hand or finger on the jaw and hold it down so you can feel the action of the tongue being isolated from the action of the jaw. It is not necessary to go too high—maybe for a mezzo or baritone, to an F above the staff, and for a tenor or soprano, up to around a G above the staff. In this exercise, you are isolating the action of the tongue from the jaw. This is very important in loosening up the tongue so you are not dependent on the tongue to hold notes for you. You realize that it is the release and use of the breath that holds the tone out for you.

It is hard to explain in writing how to accomplish these exercises, but there is little that you, as a student, can do wrong, so go ahead and try them. With the CD you should be able to follow along and get the idea of how to apply these exercises in your practice time. I hope that you, as students and readers, will believe me and try these ideas out for a while. By that I mean three or four times a week for a couple of months.

No 8. - Going on to the next exercise in my training. I do caution you to be careful with this one. I am reluctant to include it, but I know how much tension it can release, so I will explain it and show you how to do it. Since I have always felt like I was on the cutting edge of vocal training, I will go ahead and let you, the student or teacher, try it out.

In the female voice, I refer to using a "Marilyn Monroe" type of sound. Very breathy, soft, and no tension. Kind of high-pitched also. In case any of you have developed throat tension or muscular tension, this is a way of alleviating it. So, on notes like E-flat-F-G-F-E-flat, do very breathy "mee-meh-mah-moh-moo." Sound like Marilyn. Then follow it with the same notes and progressions, but add firmness to the tone—more like you were singing it mezzo forte, meaning medium volume. Keeping in mind the feeling and placement of the soft and breathy progression. What this does is release tension in the throat and allow the breath, not the muscle, to support the sound. Try to almost run out of breath on the soft part of the exercise. Then breathe in again and sing it more fully (you will hear this demonstrated on the CD). The reason this can be dangerous, if done for a long period of time, is that you are separating the vocal cords, and that is not the way you sing. However, done as an exercise once a day,

I have found that the release of throat tension overshadows the danger. Remember to do this exercise only once in your warm-up. You can move these three notes up and back, going low and high. It becomes more difficult to make a breathy sound up high, so only take it, male or female, as high as a G above the staff. THEN STOP!

This exercise is mainly for people with a great deal of tension in their throat. Some people need not do it at all. It is your choice. So many teachers insist on a pure, clean, non-breathy sound in the beginning of building a technique. I have found that the natural sound in an undeveloped instrument will be somewhat breathy and light. That is as it should be. Leave it alone and with correct vocal work, the sound becomes clear and pure. It doesn't take too long for that to happen naturally. My advice is to leave the voice alone as much as possible and simply stretch and strengthen it until you begin to feel some control over the flow of the sound.

The same rule applies to the use of the breath. Many students complain that they don't have enough breath to get through a phrase comfortably or to hold out the last note of a song. My answer to that may seem simplistic, but I will share it with you anyway. My belief in the function of the breath in singing is that the more you use the breath, the more you will develop it. I do not believe you will develop more breath capacity by holding the breath. By using it, you create more space for a longer breath to be utilized. As the mechanism itself develops more power and strength, you will find that you do not waste or lose as much air and, therefore, you have more air to use. It is a simple law.

No. 9 - After that exercise, I try to put in another light "patter" type to release any tension that might have built up during the previous exercise. So we might do another tongue twister like "clickity-clickity-clickity-clickity-clack." Same notes as on the "kiddily-kit" exercise. Simply a triad up and down, such as C-E-G-E-C. Now this is an extension of the "kiddily kit," and you will find it harder to do if you have any tongue tension. If you have done lots of speech exercises, it will not be a problem for you. If not, it will take some time to build up to doing the exercise fast and with agility. Now that the voice is relaxed, we can go on to something a little more vocally demanding.

There are three types of tapes that I have used over the last thirty-five years or more of teaching. One is the warm-up tape, which should be used when performing a show or concert, and another is a work tape to be used when you are not performing every day. The last one is the warm-down tape, which is used after a performance and before you retire for the night. We will get into that one a little later in this chapter.

No. 10 - Continuing with the basic warm-up tape, I would move into what I call the "mellow-mellow" exercise. Everyone—well, almost everyone—loves this vocal exercise. Meryl Streep and many others love it, so it must be good. It does help to open up the resonators and place the tone in a very buzzy place. We do love a buzzy sound. So, starting around G above middle C, we move down in thirds. I like to start this exercise on a hum on G and then open to a sung "mel-" on the same G. Then sing "-low" on E, "mel-" on F, "-low" on D, and back to "mel-" on E. Then sing "-low" on C, "mel-" on D, "-low" on B, and the whole word "mellow" on C. (This is complicated to read, but once you hear it on the CD, it will all make sense.) I like to start this exercise with a hum because it places the voice where it belongs to sing the words. Remember to make the hum a nose hum and not a throat hum. Moving down by half steps again, go as low as is comfortable—probably low G or F below middle C. Then, starting in the middle again at G, do the same thing and move up by half steps until you are in the total head register—sopranos to around B-flat, mezzos and baritones to G.

That is my basic warm-up for working with a new student. Many variations for these and other more difficult exercises are available as the student progresses in understanding their own voice and its capabilities. However, this is a good starting point.

No. 11 - Sometimes I like to finish the warm-up with just a "yah-yah-yah-yah-yah-yah-yah." This is done on an arpeggio for one octave, up and down. Starting at G below middle C, sing G-B-D-G-D-B-G—a "yah" on every note. The tongue and the jaw are moving together on this exercise. It allows you to let go of all the concentration of the lesson and to release the mental and physical tensions of the warm-up. While doing this last freeing exercise, just jump up and down, run around the room, lean over, and swing arms—anything you can do physically to let go. It feels great!

You can vary some of these vocal exercises for yourself, so be my guest and experiment. It is your instrument and your responsibility to know how it works. All a teacher should do is guide you into the correct usage of the laws that govern the singing voice. There are certain undeniable laws involved here, and I think the closer we stick to these laws, the more success the student has in their singing career. I would, again, equate these laws to the dancer. There are certainly many physical laws governing the dancer's technique, and if not followed, can result in dangerous injuries. These laws have to be learned and obeyed. I believe the singer can and does do injury to their instrument if they do not obey the basic laws involved in good singing technique. Observe the singers who develop nodes, nodules, and broken blood vessels in the throat. These problems generally occur when the laws are not followed and obeyed. You can get away with a certain amount of bad technique, but eventually it will catch up with you and then you will have to take the time out to fix whatever the problem is—or quit singing. Not a great choice.

## WARM-DOWN TAPE

Let me explain the warm-down tape. When you belt or sing hard for a two and a half hour show, your voice is tired afterward—especially by Saturday night and the Sunday matinee. So I have suggested to my students and performers that after the show, or before going to sleep, they take five or seven minutes and do some light vocalizing. This would include the "octave slide down" over just a medium range (not too high). No need to stretch the voice now. Then some "kiddily kits" to loosen the tongue, and a simple "mee-meh-mah" up and down three notes. Lightly, lightly, lightly.

Some people do not seem to understand what "lightly" means, so I will say it means to sing more softly and with less volume and pressure. (This is what I tell Bette Midler all the time.) Then a few "eh-ahs" again to loosen the back of the tongue from the voice box. Just a few up and down, on three notes instead of five. Finish with some "mellow-mellow" in the midrange. You will be protecting your instrument from staying in a tense position while you are sleeping. Believe me, the voice will feel much better and more fresh in the morning than if you forget to do your warm-down exercises. I usually put these few things at the end of the warm-up tape so that it is in position after the performance to just switch it on. So try it and see if I am really helping you save your voice.

## END OF WARM-DOWN TAPE

Getting back to the breathing apparatus for a moment, I would like to explain what I feel is important for the student to know. To my mind, one of the worst things a student can be taught is to "hold" their breath. If you are not using up the breath in a phrase of music, then you are not "using" the breath to sustain the sound. Letting the breath flow with the sound keeps tension out of the throat and the body. Holding the breath sets up extrinsic and intrinsic muscle tension. By extrinsic I mean the large muscles such as the tongue and the jaw. By intrinsic I mean the smaller more delicate inside muscles that need to be developed.

Looking at the music from *The Secret Garden*, you really need to be able to connect note to note and word to word. Not notes punched one by one or words punched one by one. That might not apply to a show like *Rent*, but that is not my idea of correct vocal singing. A show like *Wicked* is very hard on the extended range of the middle voice.

I believe that you can all accomplish a great deal of vocal improvement and ease of singing by following these exercises for an extended period of time. I wish all my readers much joy and success in your singing careers.

# ♪ APPENDIX II ♫

Vocal Health Guidelines
and Articles

♪

## Vocal Trouble Signs

The following signs, if they persist, are indications that you should see an otolaryngologist who is a specialist in dealing with voice disorders. Always check with your voice teacher before going to any throat doctor.

1. Hoarseness which lasts more than a few weeks.

2. Excessive fatigue after singing.

3. Reduced endurance.

4. Reduced vocal range and/or volume.

5. "Breaks" in the voice, places where notes seem to cut out.

6. A change of voice quality in part or all of the range.

7. Pain during or after singing.

8. Tenderness upon palpitation around the larynx and/or the strap muscles which surround it.

9. Reflux symptoms, such as poor speaking voice quality, lowered speaking pitch, hoarseness, pain, heartburn, globus sensation in the throat, lots of throat clearing.

Do You Hear What I Hear

Massachusetts Eye and Ear Infirmary
Voice and speech laboratory
Boston, MA 02114
617-573-4050

**Guidelines for Vocal Hygiene**

Vocal use:

1. Avoid unnecessary talking, yelling, and screaming.

2. Avoid speaking in noisy environments.

3. When talking over noise or to individuals who have hearing loss, speak more slowly, face the person, and use precise articulation.

4. Avoid talking to someone from a distance or from another room. Go to them, or have them come to you.

5. If speaking before a group of people, use a microphone or get as close to the audience as possible. Again, use a slow rate and overarticulate.

6. Avoid speaking in stressful situations or when you are overly tense.

7. Don't lie down and talk on the phone.

8. Avoid coughing and throat-clearing. If you sense a buildup of secretions in the throat, try swallowing or taking a sip of water. You can also use a "silent cough"—push as much air as you can from the lungs in a short blast. The only sound should be a rush of air. Then swallow.

9. Use your voice minimally if you have a bad cold or laryngitis.

10. Avoid whispering!!!

11. Avoid making non-speech noises such as engine or animal noises.

12. Avoid speaking too long on one breath. Take frequent pauses to replenish your air in order to avoid squeezing with your throat.

13. Women should be especially careful to limit vocal demands and abusive behaviors just prior to and during the menstrual cycle. The lowering of estrogen levels just before menses can result in increased vocal fold edema in some women.

## Nonuse-Related Factors

1. Get adequate sleep/rest. When you are tired, you are more likely to strain your voice.

2. Drink plenty of water. Eight 8-ounce glasses a day is recommended. Water helps to hydrate the vocal folds and to thin secretions that can irritate the folds and/or make you feel like you need to clear your throat.

3. Maintain adequate humidity to avoid dryness. If you have forced-air heat, try using a humidifier at night.

4. Avoid the following drying agents:
   a. Caffeine
   b. Alcohol
   c. Antihistamines (unless prescribed by your doctor)

5. Avoid aspirin, unless prescribed. Use an aspirin substitute such as Tylenol.

6. Don't smoke. Avoid smoky environments. Cigarette smoke is hot and dry and easily irritates the vocal folds.

7. Avoid milk, chocolate, and other dairy products if you have problems with excess mucous.

8. Avoid spicy foods, eating late at night, and lying down after eating to reduce the likelihood of gastric reflux (stomach acid coming up from your stomach into the back of your throat, which can irritate the vocal folds).

I believe that all of these recommendations apply to the singer as well as any person who uses their voice professionally.

## Some Questions You Might Ask a Voice Teacher

*What do you believe to be the most important aspect of your teaching?*

1. Can you build a voice from the beginning stages?

2. Do you have preconceived ideas of what a new student is capable or incapable of accomplishing with their voice?

3. Do you treat dancers taking singing lessons differently than you treat singers? This would apply to piano players also.

4. If an individual's voice has been damaged, what is your method of repairing that voice? What exercises, how much work, how much rest, how much time.

5. Do you have your students checked by a laryngologist (throat doctor) if you hear anything unusual in their production?

6. What is your teaching routine? Half-hour lessons, 45-minute lessons or 1-hour lessons? Do you help with songs or just technique? Do you work particularly difficult notes or areas of a song with the student?

7. Do you demonstrate with your own voice how an exercise or phrase should be done or do you explain the proper way and let the student find how to do it?

8. How do you determine "range"? Do you believe in the singing voice being an extension of the speaking voice?

9. How do you relate the male voice to the female voice—in registers?

10. Do you try to extend the student's range—both upper and lower?

These questions were put to me as an introduction to a seminar to be filmed on what I believed was important as a teacher.

## Can the Voice Do It All?

*For singers and actors alike, today's vocal demands are greater than ever. How do we stay vocally healthy and make director, playwright, composer and audience happy?*

Article by Marge Rivingston

Appeared in AFTRA's 50th anniversary magazine ~ September, 1987

In the entertainment business today a performer is required to be facile enough to encompass a whole range of vocal abilities. As a singer, you must be able to produce a belt sound that will fit a score like *Evita* (both the male and female leads), a mixed belt sound for older musicals such as *South Pacific* and a truly female soprano sound for scores like *Oklahoma*, in its era, and Rosa Bud in *Drood* today. For the male voice things are a bit easier, but in the rock musicals you must have a very well developed falsetto or head voice that can be mixed with the chest voice. A good example today is *Les Miserables* (Jean Valjean). These are just a few requirements that confuse the voice teacher, the students, the musical directors and, I guess, everyone else with the exception of the composers who hear in their heads the sound they want for a particular piece.

Approaching the voice of the actor, things are also difficult. Accents tend to put muscle tension in the vocal mechanism, whining nasal sounds close off air passages, deep resonant bass sounds cut off the head resonances and tend to thicken the chords. Crying or emotional scenes close the throat and stop the air from moving and tighten throat muscles. Shouting thickens the cords if not done properly, from the diaphragm. Overarticulation to be understood (by both actors and singers) places undue pressure on the tongue and lips.

So where do we go from here? How do we stay vocally healthy and make everyone happy: director, playwright, composer and audience most of all?

♪

Some basic laws apply, and I firmly believe in simple exercises that relax the inevitable tensions one encounters, particularly during learning and rehearsal periods.

Here are some I recommend:

Starting with vocal stretching, try opening like a yawn when breathing in and sigh through an octave (eg: g to g): go on up the scale by half tones until you have stretched the soft palate as far as it will go. Pitch is not important, so you can do this exercise with speech sound too – from up to down, then back up and down again, continuing as high as possible into the head voice.

During *all* vocal exercises make sure the shoulders and chest are not involved in the breathing – a straight pipe line from diaphragm through the mouth. Check in the mirror to make sure you see and feel what you are doing. Actors and singers tend to be shy about looking at themselves while practicing. Dancers understand much better how they look when they are performing; they grow up watching their bodies in the mirror. After all, the audience has to look at you; let's make it pleasant.

Next try warming up the facial muscles with going back and forth on one pitch just a comfortable mid range one on "ee" (spread mouth like a grin) and "oo" (closing lips to form "oo".) Do this back and forth, "ee-oo, ee-oo, ee-oo,ee-oo" and then open to an "ah" vowel by just dropping the jaw and keeping the resonance where you feel it on the "ee" vowel. Go up a little in pitch and down, always starting in the middle of the voice and moving it up and down from the middle. These first two exercises are done with very little sound: do not press for a loud sound too soon in warming up. Think of dancers and their slow stretching.

The third thing is to exercise the tongue so it is free in the back of the throat and where it is attached to the larynx. Open the jaw and hold it down with your hand, relax tongue against back of the bottom teeth and use the vowels "eh ah, eh ah, eh ah" – tongue goes up in the back on the "eh" and down on the "ah". Up and down, not in and out. I am not advocating a low tongue position for an "ah " vowel, but only using this idea to exercise the tongue. Use a five note scale (eg: cdefg and down fedc) doing "eh" on c, "ah" on d, "eh" on e, "ah" on f and so forth, on the last c do "eh-ah" and hold. You can also just do the exercise on a speaking sound. Make sure no glottal attacks. Do not use a lot of volume yet.

Lots of people feel good warming up with a humming sound. Try a hum, and when the sinus resonators are open sing or speak the word "mellow' – mellow, mellow, mellow, mellow, again keeping the same resonance feeling as with the hum. If you feel air coming through the nostrils you will be assured of an open hum, not a tight closed one.

Staccatos or sharp short sounds are excellent for the development of placement of sound. Taking the vowels "ah oh eh ee ah" and making them very percussive sounding, connects the diaphragm, the sound and the breath in one coordinated effort. These three things should happen simultaneously. Now, try it. Breathe first, then on the first staccato pull the stomach in. (Do not push it out, as that results in a pushed sound going down, and we want the sound moving up and out the mouth.) Do these in the middle of the vocal range then down a few and up a few; not too extended in range either direction; each vowel a new staccato "ah-oh-eh-ee-ah".

The falsetto or head voice is difficult to explain but in trying to find it easily try to keep the sound light and soft. Do not try to take lots of lower register sound into a high sound. There are natural transitions for the voice to make and it must be loose and free enough muscularly to make these changes by itself. I often say to my students, "Why don't you let your voice tell you how it would like to sing once in a while, instead of you telling it how to do it all the time". The voice is a marvelous individualistic instrument and we get too caught up in thinking we have to sound a certain way, instead of letting our natural sound speak for us. My belief is that there are four transitions as the voice goes up and down. In singing: lower register, lower middle, upper middle and upper or in a case of really high coloratura (like Maureen Mc Govern) a fifth-place of pure upper register sound. These transitions should be smooth but as we have all heard in performances, this is rarely the case.

On breath control, I believe that isolated breathing exercises do not really help the development of the sound or breath support. The only way is to connect some sound with the breathing work. The old idea of the "bellows" effect is still very good. Expand when taking in air (watch the shoulders and chest) and , using it on a phrase of singing or a long sentence, let the ribs and diaphragm actually relax. It is very difficult to get a new fresh breath in for the next phrase or sentence if you are holding breath in rigidly. If you hold the breath to conserve it, you have no use of it and you must use throat, neck, shoulder or whatever muscle tensions to produce the sound. The sound should ride on top of the column of air, and if you constantly use the air it will develop its capacity for long phrases by itself. But always use some sound connected to the breath to practice this. (So much for some practical ideas and applications.)

What about the classic versus television and other microphone-type speaking or singing? The projection of a classical voice without amplification must be free to express dynamic changes, to project to the back row and to articulate. We are now involved, even on stage, with so much microphone technique that it is hard to be able to move from one to the other comfortably.

Having no amplification means energy and sound must link up to provide the necessary volume to carry through the theater. But with amplification I have found that the biggest problem actors and singers find is how to keep the energy of the character without pushing the voice. Knowing that the projection is taken care of tends to make the performer's energy dissipate. The aim is to keep the live energy and not push the sound too much. This result should make it easier vocally for the actor or singer, but it is another technique to be learned in order to keep the emotion of the character alive and honest.

Well, these are some of my personal ideas for the development and health of the vocal mechanism. We have a magnificent instrument at our disposal to communicate. Recently, I was speaking with Florence

Norberg, a London voice teacher, and she made a statement that pulled me up short with its clarity and focus. She said: "The voice is the only instrument that cannot be replaced. We should have more respect for it!" We do tend to abuse our voices and expect them to last through it all. It is a bit of an unreasonable request.

ISBN 142512020-2

9 781425 120207